Inner Peace, World Peace

SUNY Series in Buddhist Studies
Matthew Kapstein, Editor

Inner Peace, World Peace
Essays on Buddhism and Nonviolence

Edited by Kenneth Kraft

STATE UNIVERSITY OF NEW YORK PRESS

An earlier version of the chapter entitled "Nonviolence to Animals in Buddhism and Jainism," by Christopher Chapple, originally appeared in Tom Regan, ed., *Animal Sacrifices: Religious Perspectives on the Use of Animals in Science* (Philadelphia: Temple University Press, 1986); copyright © by Temple University. The present version has been reprinted by permission of Temple University Press. Grateful acknowledgment is made to the Library of Tibetan Works and Archives, Dharamsala, India, for permission to reprint from *A Prayer of Words of Truth* (1975), by His Holiness the Dalai Lama.

Published by
State University of New York Press, Albany

© 1992 by Kenneth Kraft

For information, address State University of New York Press,
90 State Street, Suite 700, Albany NY 12207

Production by Cathleen Collins
Marketing by Bernadette LaManna

Library of Congress Cataloging-in-Publication Data

Inner peace, world peace : essays on Buddhism and nonviolence / edited
  by Kenneth Kraft.
      p.   cm. — (SUNY series in Buddhist studies)
    Includes bibliographical references and index.
    ISBN 0-7914-0969-4 — ISBN 0-7914-0970-8 (pbk.)
    1. Peace—Religious aspects—Buddhism.   2. Nonviolence—Religious
  aspects—Buddhism.   3. Buddhism—Social aspects.   I. Kraft, Kenneth
  Lewis.   II. Series
BQ4570.P4166   1992   91-3425
294.3'5697—dc20   CIP

10 9 8 7 6 5 4 3 2

Contents

Acknowledgments

Without the generous assistance of many people and several institutions, this book would never have been published. Philip Kapleau responded keenly to the original proposal, and a grant from the Rochester Zen Center put the project in motion. Crucial support was received from Kenneth Inada, Arnold Kotler, Martin Collcutt, Audrey Fernandez, Greg Mello, Thomas Roberts, and Trudy Kraft. Sōgen Hori, Robert Sharf, Harold Abilock, Donald Rothberg, and Stephen Miller kindly read portions of the manuscript. Michael Kohn offered valuable editorial suggestions, and Mitra Bishop retyped numerous drafts. Final revisions were made during a sabbatical leave in Kyoto, supported by the Japan Foundation and the International Research Institute for Zen Buddhism, Hanazono University.

Introduction

by Kenneth Kraft

Buddhism has long been associated with peace and nonviolence. A carved or painted figure of a buddha meditating serenely in a cross-legged posture is widely recognized as an expression of inner and outer harmony. The cardinal precept of Buddhism is not to harm or kill, but to cherish all life. Though Buddhists have at times sought to achieve their goals by less than peaceful means, no major war has been fought in the name of Buddhism. History has recorded few Buddhist crusades or inquisitions. In 1989 the connection between Buddhism and nonviolence was heralded by the presentation of the Nobel Peace Prize to the Dalai Lama, exiled Buddhist leader of Tibet. Since Tibet's occupation by China over thirty years ago, the Dalai Lama has consistently advocated nonviolent solutions to his country's plight.

While a link between Buddhism and nonviolence is generally acknowledged, the broader implications of this double theme have rarely been explored in a substantive way. What are the origins of Buddhism's approach to nonviolence? What happens when theories of nonviolence are applied to actual situations? What resources might Buddhism have to offer those who confront violence or injustice today? Have the principal terms (such as "nonviolence," "peace," "Buddhism") been adequately defined? These and similar questions prompted the present volume. In the following essays the topic is explored from various perspectives, and the conclusions that emerge are far from uniform. For example, one contributor expresses some doubt about the centrality of nonviolence in

1

Buddhism. Another focuses on forms of nonviolent behavior that do not presuppose any religious base. A third argues that traditional Buddhist notions of nonviolence must be expanded greatly in light of current social conditions.

One common starting-point for Buddhist treatments of this subject is the conviction that all things, near and far, are fundamentally related. Buddhism further asserts that the distinctions we make between an individual and the universe, while provisionally useful, are ultimately illusory. From this premise it follows that a single person who experiences peace of mind, or who lives in a nonviolent manner, is contributing to the peace of the world. A few months before receiving the Nobel Prize, the Dalai Lama declared:

> The question of real, lasting world peace concerns human beings, so basic human feelings are also at its roots. Through inner peace, genuine world peace can be achieved. In this the importance of individual responsibility is quite clear; an atmosphere of peace must first be created within ourselves, then gradually expanded to include our families, our communities, and ultimately the whole planet.[1]

Some Buddhist teachings claim that the mind does not just affect the world, it actually creates and sustains it. According to this view, cosmic harmony is most effectively preserved through an individual's spiritual practice. Yet other Buddhists amend the notion that mind is the primary or exclusive source of peace, contending that inner serenity is fostered or impeded by external conditions. "Without freedom from want and oppression, people cannot be expected to appreciate more sublime forms of personal liberation," writes Sulak Sivaraksa in these pages. Buddhists who place importance upon social factors and social action believe that internal transformation cannot, by itself, quell the world's turbulence.

The advent of Buddhists who are concerned about world peace and other sociopolitical issues is itself a topic that invites attention. Isn't Buddhism an inwardly focused religion that gives precedence to meditation over any kind of social activity? Isn't it contradictory to speak of a "socially engaged Buddhism"? While the heart of the tradition may indeed be a solitary spiritual quest, Buddhism also displays remarkable diversity, and there is increasing recognition of the ways in which Buddhists and their institutions become involved in the world.

Both sides of this theme—engagement and disengagement—are explored in this collection of essays. According to one important strain of early Buddhist thought, nonviolence was conceived primarily in terms of abstention. As Luis Gómez demonstrates in his chapter, a monk was supposed to uphold the precept against harming other beings by carefully avoiding certain kinds of behavior. The standards were quite high, but the point is that abstention alone was enough—there was no further injunction to extend the practice of nonviolence to some wider social realm. A more contemporary image of Buddhism's apparent unworldliness can be found in a remote monastery in the forests of southern Thailand, where the respected master Buddhadasa has been meditating and teaching for over fifty years. Depicted in Donald Swearer's essay as an exemplar of nonviolence, Buddhadasa lectures at dawn under his favorite tree, gently brushing aside the chickens that hop onto his lap.

Understandably, Buddhism often appears to promote personal transformation at the expense of social concern. A recent study reiterates the accepted view: "What unifying element there is in Buddhism, Mahayana and non-Mahayana, is provided by the monks and their adherence to the monastic rule."[2] In China, countless generations of Confucianists accused Buddhists of withdrawing from the world out of selfishness. Wang Yangming (1472–1529) charged that Buddhists were "afraid of the troubles involved in the relationships between father and son, ruler and subject, and husband and wife; therefore [they] escape from these relationships."[3] In Japan, Buddhism is commonly faulted for becoming too subservient to the state. Assessing Buddhism during the Tokugawa era (1603–1867), a modern Japanese historian concluded:

> With the establishment of [Tokugawa] feudal organization, Buddhist circles capitulated to secular power, willingly fulfilled the task of safeguarding the status quo, and gave up all of their noteworthy social functions.[4]

D. T. Suzuki, ordinarily a defender of Zen, did not exalt its role in the sociopolitical realm: "[Zen] may be found wedded to anarchism or fascism, communism or democracy . . . or any political or economic dogmatism."[5] Most Western scholars have also tended to perceive Buddhism as world-denying, passive, or socially inept. Max Weber was one of the first to declare that Buddhist devotees carry the "asocial character of genuine mysticism . . . to its maximum."[6]

Yet there are other specialists, including several of the contributors to this volume, who have begun to question such interpretations. Instead they perceive in Buddhism a creative tension between withdrawal and involvement, an underlying synonymity between work on oneself and work on behalf of others. Evidence supporting this viewpoint is found in doctrine, in practice, in legend, and in history. Thus the preeminent virtues in Theravada Buddhism are self-restraint *and* generosity; in Mahayana Buddhism, the highest goals are wisdom *and* compassion.

It is noteworthy, in this regard, that the story of the Buddha's spiritual journey climaxes with his enlightenment but does not end there. Even as he was savoring the blissful state that followed his awakening, he was approached (in the traditional account) by a delegation of gods, who begged him to give up his private ecstasy so he could share his awakening with those who still suffered. This encounter and its outcome, however legendary, make the point that spiritual maturity includes the ability to actualize transcendent insight in daily life. The Buddha is said to have wandered across northern India for forty years, tirelessly teaching the Dharma. His decision to arise from his seat under the Bo tree and go out into the world can be considered the first step of a socially engaged Buddhism. The Buddha's discourses, which had revolutionary force in the society of his time, include countless passages dealing with "this-worldly" topics such as politics, good government, poverty, crime, war, peace, and ecology.[7]

When Buddhism is no longer assumed to be world-rejecting, several aspects of the tradition acquire new significance. For example, Robert Thurman argues in his chapter on Tibet that the Buddhist monastic community (the Sangha) represents a consciously planned social movement, a "nonviolent army of peace." The great Indian king Aśoka (third century B.C.E.), who figures in several of the essays, apparently sought to demonstrate that an entire country could be ruled in accord with Buddhist principles. By promoting nonviolent domestic and foreign policies, Aśoka extended the doctrine of nonviolence to include the notion of social harmony. Even Nāgārjuna (second century C.E.), the great Buddhist dialectician, is said to have outlined the kind of society that would accord with Buddhism's basic tenets.[8]

Among the contemporary figures who personify Buddhism's active dimensions is the Vietnamese Zen master Thich Nhat Hanh, who gained international recognition for his efforts to end the Vietnam War. Today Nhat Hanh is working creatively with Buddhists and non-Buddhists throughout North America and Europe, teaching new ways of "being peace." He maintains that individual serenity should not be sought in isolation from the world:

> The peace we seek cannot be our personal possession. We need to find an inner peace which makes it possible for us to become one with those who suffer, and to do something to help our brothers and sisters, which is to say, ourselves. . . . This peace is not a barricade which separates you from the world. On the contrary, this kind of peace brings you into the world and empowers you to undertake whatever you want to do to try to help.[9]

A socially engaged Buddhism raises many questions that will continue to stimulate discussion and reflection. For instance, is it necessary to prove that engagement was an integral feature of original Buddhism, or is it enough to demonstrate that it can be derived naturally from Buddhism's past? What are the differences between Buddhist-inspired activism and activism that arises from other religious or secular belief-systems? A number of challenging practical issues also emerge: Is it possible to become involved without becoming attached? Must one be partially or fully enlightened before one can act in the world with true wisdom and compassion? Such topics are of particular concern to Buddhism's new adherents in the West, as Cynthia Eller shows in her comparison of Buddhist and Christian social ethics.

Another question that often arises is whether a person who embraces nonviolence is entitled to resort to violence in extreme situations—such as self-defense, defense of innocent people, or defense of one's country. Different answers are found in the various streams of the Buddhist tradition. Though certain scriptural passages contend that a Buddhist "must not hate any being and cannot kill a living creature even in thought,"[10] one influential sutra states that in order to protect the truth of Buddhism it may be necessary to bear arms and ignore the moral code.[11] The *Jātaka* tales depict saintly figures who calmly allow themselves to be hacked to pieces, yet other canonical sources advise kings to mobilize their troops against invaders. Certain schools refrain from addressing such issues theoretically; instead they claim that people who have trained themselves to live each day consciously and nonviolently will intuitively know how to react in a given situation.

One commendable response to an imminent attack is illustrated in a Zen anecdote:

> When a rebel army swept into a town in Korea, all the monks of the Zen temple fled except for the abbot. The general came into the temple and was annoyed that the abbot did not receive him with respect. "Don't you know," he shouted, "that you are looking at a man who can run you through without blinking?" "And you," replied the abbot strongly, "are looking at a man who can be run through without blinking!" The general stared at him, then made a bow and retired.[12]

A similar confrontation that occurred recently in Burma is recounted in Chapter 1. But for most of us, to puzzle over such uncommon scenarios is to leap too quickly to abstract speculation. Ordinarily, no clear-cut boundary separates nonviolent and violent behavior, and it is impossible to adhere to an absolute standard (we kill tiny beings whenever we boil water). Thus the ideal of nonviolence is more a direction than a fixed position.

Many Buddhists recognize that a kind of violence is sometimes necessary to prevent a greater violence. The Dalai Lama tells a story about two monks sitting beside a rain-swollen river, waiting for an evening ferry. A man who is quite drunk suddenly steps off the bank and begins to wade into the strong current, oblivious to the danger. One of the monks runs over and tries to pull him back, but the drunken man resists violently, until the monk's only recourse is to knock the man out. In such a case, comments the Dalai Lama, the monk who sat still and did nothing behaved more violently than the monk who subdued the drunk by force. Because motive and intention play a critical role, certain formulations can become a slippery slope. A compassionate person may even be compelled to kill someone, wrote Asaṅga in the fourth century C.E., if that is the only way to save the lives of many others.[13] In highly charged situations that may lead to killing, only those with the spiritual development of a buddha are deemed capable of deliberately abrogating the principle of nonviolence; the Dalai Lama declines to put himself in that category.[14]

A feature that originally set Buddhism apart from Hinduism, and that still characterizes it in several cultures, is an expressed opposition to the slaughter of animals. Rather than making a sharp distinction between humans and animals, Buddhism groups them together as "sentient beings," subject equally to birth and death, pain and fear. According to the doctrine of karma, people can be reborn as animals, and animals can be reborn as people, so one's past or future relatives might turn up in the most unlikely places. Hence the adoption of vegetarianism by certain Buddhists. Asian Buddhists ceremonially liberate animals in captivity, buying them from breeders or pet stores and releasing them back to their natural environments. (An American Zen center celebrates Thanksgiving by freeing turkeys.) Christopher Chapple notes in his essay that Buddhists are beginning to express concern about the treatment of animals in other contemporary contexts, including laboratory experiments.

In cases such as the treatment of animals in scientific research, classic Buddhist tenets are being applied to situations that differ greatly from the contexts in which those tenets were originally conceived. The Buddhist creed of nonviolence that once functioned as a personal moral code for monks in ancient India is now expected to provide guidelines for dealing with complex social and political dilemmas. Though such leaps may seem dubious from certain scholarly or religious standpoints, they are earnestly being attempted nonetheless. Graphic reminders of the discrepancies between ancient and modern worldviews are furnished by the traditional stories cited in these pages. An elephant sacrifices himself for a rabbit, a human prince sacrifices himself for a tigress, a merchant has an inexhaustible rice pot, a celestial savior is reconstituted from a thousand fragments, and so on. Here such accounts are examined principally for their doctrinal implications, though that is only one of the perspectives from which they can be viewed. Whatever complexities have been engendered by changing historical conditions, certain fundamental principles have remained constant for Buddhist believers.

A significant Buddhist interpretation of nonviolence concerns the application of that ideal to daily life. Nonviolence is not some exalted regimen that can be practiced only by a monk or a master; it also pertains to the way one interacts with a child, vacuums a carpet, or waits in line. Besides the more obvious forms of violence, whenever we separate ourselves from a given situation (for example, through inattentiveness, negative judgments, or impatience), we "kill" something valuable. However subtle it may be, such violence actually leaves victims in its wake: people, things, one's own composure, the moment itself. According to Buddhist reckoning, these small-scale incidences of violence accumulate relentlessly, are multiplied on a social level, and become a source of the large-scale violence that can sweep down upon us so suddenly. In contrast, any act performed with full awareness, any gesture that fosters happiness in another person, is credited as an expression of nonviolence. One need not wait until war is declared and bullets are flying to work for peace, Buddhism teaches. A more constant and equally urgent battle must be waged each day against the forces of one's own anger, carelessness, and self-absorption.

An essayist in *The New Yorker* magazine recently observed that nonviolence "ranks as one of the few great modern discoveries."[15] At first, this remark may appear short-sighted: Jainism and Buddhism have stressed nonviolence for millennia, and the Sermon on the Mount was not preached last Sunday. Yet the point is well taken. The twentieth century has witnessed Gandhi's nonviolent expulsion of the British Raj in India, Martin Luther King's nonviolent civil rights movement in the United States, and the nonviolent reversals of Communist party power in Europe and the Soviet Union. Though we tend to associate the concept of nonviolence with ancient Asian thought, some of the most notable instances of nonviolent political action have occurred in the West during this century.

Gene Sharp argues in his essay that the political potential of this "modern" discovery has yet to be fully appreciated. He believes that it may be possible to train entire populations to resist invaders or oppressors without resorting to violence, even if no one embraces pacifism philosophically or religiously. While recent events in Europe and elsewhere seem to lend credence to such assertions, important questions remain. What about someone like Hitler, or the Chinese hardliners who ordered the tanks into Tiananmen Square, or a belligerent Saddam Hussein? Are nonviolent methods effective only if one is dealing with an opponent who has a conscience? If a nonviolent movement attains a specific end (such as the removal of a dictator), has it triumphed? Or is the conversion of an entire society to a nonviolent way of life the one true measure of success? Without denying the philosophical issues involved, Sharp contends that nonviolent action must also be studied empirically, and he has been instrumental in developing a new field of research based on this approach.

These are subjects that tend to yield paradoxical conclusions. If struggle is inherent in growth and creativity, then nonviolence cannot mean the complete eradication of conflict. When a child gleefully smashes a tower of blocks, can that act of destruction also be considered a form of creation? In order for something to live, something else must usually die, so the precept to cherish all life may, from certain perspectives, imply a reverence for death as well. Yet Buddhists who recognize such paradoxes are nonetheless moved to alleviate suffering and promote peace. Poet Gary Snyder, a long-time student of Zen, reflects:

> I'm still trying to understand, as I always will be, the many levels of the meaning of the first Buddhist precept: not to be harmful, not to harm.... We mustn't be dualistic even about war and peace, or about warlikeness and peacefulness. Peace contains war, war contains peace. In any situation, in any place, in any condition, even in the battle right in the middle of the war, you must appreciate and be grateful for the little bit of nonviolence or a little bit of less harmfulness or intelligent nonharmfulness that might be practiced there. And we must be alert in a parallel way in the realm of peace to the kinds of aggression that take place.[16]

Notes

1. The Dalai Lama, Address in San Jose, Costa Rica, June 1989, *Buddhist Peace Fellowship Newsletter* (Fall 1989), 4.
2. Paul Williams, *Mahāyāna Buddhism* (London: Routledge, 1989), 4.
3. Fung Yu-lan, *A History of Chinese Philosophy*, vol. 2 (Princeton: Princeton University Press, 1973), 610–11.
4. Ienaga Saburo, "Japan's Modernization and Buddhism," in *Contemporary Religions in Japan* (International Institute for the Study of Religions, Tokyo) 6:1 (March 1965).
5. D. T. Suzuki, *Zen and Japanese Culture* (Princeton: Princeton University Press, 1973), 63.
6. Max Weber, *The Religion of India*, trans. Hans H. Gerth and Don Martindale (New York: The Free Press, 1958), 213.
7. See, for example, Walpola Rahula, "The Social Teachings of the Buddha," in Fred Eppsteiner, ed., *The Path of Compassion: Writings on Socially Engaged Buddhism* (Berkeley: Parallax Press, 1988), 103–110; and Chatsumarn Kabilsingh, "Early Buddhist Views on Nature," in Allan Hunt Badiner, *Dharma Gaia* (Berkeley: Parallax Press, 1990), 8–13.
8. Robert A. F. Thurman, "Nagarjuna's Guidelines for Buddhist Social Activism," in Eppsteiner, *The Path of Compassion*, 120–44.
9. Thich Nhat Hanh, *The Sun My Heart* (Berkeley: Parallax Press, 1988), 127–28.

10. *Daśabhūmika Sūtra,* in Har Dayal, *The Bodhisattva Doctrine in Buddhist Sanskrit Literature* (London: Kegal Paul, Trench, Trubner, and Co., 1931), 199.
11. *Mahāparinirvāna Sūtra,* in Williams, *Mahāyāna Buddhism,* 161.
12. Trevor Leggett, *The Tiger's Cave* (London: Routledge & Kegan Paul, 1977), 160.
13. Mark Tatz, trans., *Asaṅga's Chapter on Ethics with the Commentary of Tsong-Kha-Pa, The Basic Path to Awakening, the Complete Bodhisattva,* by Bodhisattva Yogacarabhumi (Lewiston/Queenston: Edwin Mellen Press, 1986), 70–72.
14. Catherine Ingram, *In the Footsteps of Gandhi: Conversations with Spiritual Social Activists* (Berkeley: Parallax Press, 1990), 13.
15. "Talk of the Town," *The New Yorker,* 12 December 1983, 43.
16. Gary Snyder, et al., "The Warrior and the Militarist: A Discussion," in *The Sun* 125 (April 1986), 19.

1

Prospects of a Socially Engaged Buddhism

by Kenneth Kraft

In the spring of 1965 a Vietnamese monk named Thich Nhat Hanh wrote an impassioned letter to Dr. Martin Luther King, Jr. It stated in part:

> Now in the confrontation of the big powers occurring in our country, hundreds and perhaps thousands of Vietnamese peasants and children lose their lives every day, and our land is unmercifully and tragically torn by a war which is already twenty years old. I am sure that since you have been engaged in one of the hardest struggles for equality and human rights, you are among those who understand fully, and who share with all their heart, the indescribable suffering of the Vietnamese people. The world's greatest humanists would not remain silent. You yourself cannot remain silent.[1]

The two men met the following year, and their relationship became a key factor in King's controversial decision to speak out against U.S. involvement in Vietnam. "You know, Martin, in Vietnam they consider you a bodhisattva," Nhat Hanh later informed his new friend. Shortly before King was assassinated, he nominated Nhat Hanh for the Nobel Peace Prize, declaring, "I do not personally know of anyone more worthy of the Nobel Peace Prize than this gentle Buddhist monk from Vietnam."[2] Though precedents for a politically responsive Buddhism can be

11

found throughout the Buddhist tradition, Thich Nhat Hanh and other contemporary figures have sparked the reemergence of a Buddhist activism that seeks to address social issues beyond the walls of a monastery. The participants in this nascent movement come from many nations, from diverse branches of Buddhism, and from different walks of life. They are monks, nuns, and laypeople, Asians, Americans, and Europeans, adherents of Mahayana, Theravada, and Vajrayana Buddhism, scholars and spiritual masters, First World homemakers and Third World insurgents. Individual agendas vary, but the ideal (at least for those who articulate ideals) is to transform oneself while transforming the world, through awareness and compassionate involvement.

One of the features that distinguishes this emerging network as "Buddhist," especially for the Westerners who are involved, is the conviction that social work entails inner work, that social change and inner change are inseparable. While other religiously motivated activists share this outlook to some degree, it seems to be applied most consistently by engaged Buddhists. A reform movement that is pursued only from a sociopolitical standpoint, they assert, will at best provide temporary solutions, and at worst it will perpetuate the very ills it aims to cure. Effective social action must also address the greed, anger, and ignorance that cripple us as groups and as individuals. Work on oneself is therefore essential, though it means different things to different Buddhists. For some, the calm awareness that is cultivated in a meditation hall can also be applied to forms of political protest that might otherwise become violent. An American who expressed opposition to the arms race by damaging parts of a Pershing II nuclear missile interpreted that deed in light of his Buddhist practice:

> Although [the action against the missile] occurred in the dimension of protest, it was not in essence an act of protest. It was an effort to do a new thing. It flowed from the understanding that these weapons are an intimate, personal problem, like an impacted wisdom tooth or a build-up of garbage under the kitchen sink. . . . We accept our own ownership of the bomb and begin the process of disarmament within and without. We tried to interact within our group sensitively, harmoniously, justly. We tried to perform our act of disarmament in perfect nonviolence and to endure the court of law and prison without rancor, for it is our hearts that must be changed. Everything depends on it.[3]

Because Buddhism is not perceived to have been socially active in Asia (at least in comparison to Christianity's role in the West), Western Buddhists have had to reassure themselves that their adopted tradition really sanctions the sociopolitical engagement to which they are drawn. The first step is to challenge those who promulgated the prevailing view. As scholar-activist Joanna Macy states, "I found that the texts which had been gathered and translated into the anthologies of Buddhist thinking by nineteenth-century Western scholars had been done by people who had already decided that Buddhism was world-rejecting and passive."[4] Contemporary interpreters interested in highlighting Buddhism's world-affirming aspects have marshalled other evidence to support their position. As Nelson Foster asserts,

> It is clear from the Pali texts, apocryphal or not, that early Buddhism was aware of itself as a force for social good. Shakyamuni appears in the Pali sutras as a peacemaker, provides guidelines for good rulership, criticizes India's caste system, emphasizes morality as the foundation of practice, and so forth. In southern Buddhism to this day, monks and nuns (and devout laypersons) play integral roles in villages and urban neighborhoods, not only as moral preceptors but also as leaders in community decision-making (i.e., politics).[5]

According to Robert Thurman, certain Mahayana texts reveal the outlines of a society that is "individualist, transcendentalist, pacifist, universalist, and socialist."[6] Carried to an extreme, such interpretations envision an ideal Buddhism too far removed from its actual historical development. But the thrust of the argument is constructive: to show that the Buddhist tradition contains untapped resources for skillful social action and peacemaking, accessible to Buddhists and non-Buddhists alike.

A principal concept that underlies most forms of engaged Buddhism is the interdependence of all existence (and nonexistence). The paper on which these words appear is the product of countless causal factors—tree, rain, cloud, logger, trucker, those who perfected the papermaking process, the fuels used to manufacture and transport the product, the sources of those fuels, and so on, endlessly. Just as a stone tossed into a still pond creates wavelets in any direction, every act—indeed every thought—is believed to have infinite repercussions in realms seen and unseen. A few drinks too many by the captain of an oil tanker may cause it to run aground, spoil many miles of coastline, ruin some local businesses but make others prosper, affect gasoline prices nationwide, create new jobs for lawyers and Congressional staffers, and so on, endlessly. Buddhist terms such as nonduality, interrelatedness, or interbeing all point to this idea. If each person is not fundamentally separate from other beings, it follows that the suffering of others is also one's own suffering, that the violence of others is also one's own violence. Christopher Titmuss, a meditation teacher active in British politics, reiterates this point:

> People are beginning to see that personal pain and global pain are not two separate factors, but very much interrelated. Some people experience inside of themselves what they conceive of as being the pain of the

world, but in a way it is the pain of themselves. There are others who experience inside of themselves what they conceive of as being purely personal pain. In a way, it is the pain of the world.[7]

This somber correlation also has a brighter side: if everything is indeed interdependent, then one individual's peace of mind contributes in a real way to peace far and near. When the Dalai Lama says, "Peace is the responsibility of everyone,"[8] he is not issuing a moral injunction; rather, he is expressing the classic Buddhist view that one affects world peace first and foremost by the way one lives.

While engaged Buddhists (and those who write about them) are repeatedly compelled to refer to "Buddhist" this and "Buddhist" that, their primary aims are not sectarian. "The movement to revive Buddhism is not for Buddhism's sake at all," says Maruyama Teruo, a Japanese priest. "We must reassess Buddhism once more in the context of problems such as the potential destruction of the human race."[9] Some movement participants are willing to dispense with the Buddhism label altogether, especially if it becomes a mark of attachment or seems to keep others at a distance; they point out that a Buddhist belief-system can be as illusory and constricting as any other belief-system. Nor is it necessary to identify oneself as a Buddhist in order to partake of the tradition's resources. For those who choose to regard themselves as Buddhists, Thich Nhat Hanh recommends a Buddhism "with a small b."

Engaged Buddhism in North America

Since the 1960s, notable developments in socially engaged Buddhism have taken place in Vietnam, Thailand, Burma, Japan, England, the United States, and elsewhere. In North America, the principal focus of this chapter, engaged Buddhism is barely two decades old, yet the foundations of an evolving movement can be identified. During the early 1970s Thich Nhat Hanh's work for peace in Vietnam attracted attention in a number of American Buddhist communities. Groups such as the Rochester Zen Center responded to the Vietnam War with all-night meditation vigils, memorial services, monthly fasts, donations to Nhat Hanh's Buddhist order, and written appeals to public officials. When Vietnam receded from the headlines, the international arms race moved higher on the agenda of Western Buddhists. In 1976 members from several centers walked across the country on behalf of nuclear disarmament, led by Japanese monks of the Nipponzan Myōhōji sect. The year 1978 marked the appearance of the Buddhist Peace Fellowship, which sought to bring "a Buddhist perspective to the peace movement, and the peace movement to the Buddhist community." Among the charter members were poet

Gary Snyder and Zen teacher Robert Aitken. The following year the Dalai Lama made his first visit to the United States and Canada. Drawing large audiences throughout his tour, he personified a model of compassionate engagement that appealed to Buddhists and non-Buddhists alike. During the 1980s, activity increased at the grassroots, national, and international levels. In the fall of 1981 another Buddhist march for peace began in San Francisco; the participants reached New York City eight months later, in time for a disarmament conference at the United Nations. For several days fifty men and women conducted a public meditation vigil at the U.N., a peace demonstration that also sought to demonstrate peace. (New York cab drivers, doubling as Zen masters, would drive by the meditators and shout "Wake up!") In 1982 the Buddhist Peace Fellowship organized its first conference on meditation and social action; since then it has sponsored dozens of workshops on similar themes. Several American Buddhist groups formed a committee in 1983 to support a U.N.-sponsored world peace center at Lumbini, the site of the Buddha's birth. In 1985 a group in Massachusetts completed the first "peace pagoda" in the Western hemisphere, an enormous white dome capped by a golden spire; nearly three thousand people attended the dedication ceremony. Another form of Buddhist social engagement was launched in the summer of 1987, when the Hartford Street Zen Center opened a hospice for AIDS patients in San Francisco. It was the first Buddhist hospice in America and the second residential hospice in San Francisco. In July 1988 fourteen American Buddhists traveled to the Soviet Union, soon after a long-standing ban on Eastern religions had been lifted. During this trip Joseph Goldstein and Sharon Salzberg introduced *vipassanā* meditation to enthusiastic gatherings in Moscow, Leningrad, and Tbilisi.

   Thich Nhat Hanh has continued to make biannual appearances in North America. His tours include various retreats designed for different groups, including peaceworkers, environmental activists, therapists, Vietnam veterans and their families, Vietnamese refugees, and children. In 1991 a retreat on the East Coast drew four hundred participants, and a lecture on the West Coast attracted an audience of four thousand. The Dalai Lama has been equally active in the United States in recent years; he was in California conferring with Western psychologists and spiritual leaders when he learned that he had won the 1989 Nobel Peace Prize. In tandem with these developments, an expanding body of literature in English has chronicled and nourished the advent of engaged Buddhism in the West.[10]

   Though Western Buddhists have only begun to explore possible avenues of spiritually inspired engagement, a number of activities and practices have already gained acceptance. For most of the Westerners, meditation heads the list. (This is not necessarily true of their Asian counterparts, as will be seen below.) Those who embrace the doctrine of interdependence believe that authentic meditation significantly affects the world: in transforming oneself, one naturally transforms others. Similarly, engaged Buddhists in North America regard most other traditional Buddhist practices—vows, chanting, repentence, and so on—as resources for aware social activism and peacemaking. While some Buddhist techniques are utilized without modification, others are adapted to reflect contemporary conditions. For example, Joanna Macy has recast a Buddhist death meditation in a nuclear context. She begins by asking her listeners to select a friend or a stranger and to imagine what might happen to that person if there were a nuclear war or accident:

> Observe that face, unique, vulnerable . . . those eyes still can see, they are not empty sockets. . . . the skin is still intact. . . . Become aware of your desire, as it arises, that this person be spared such suffering and horror, feel the strength of that desire. . . . Let the possibility arise in your consciousness that this may be the person you happen to be with when you die. . . . Open to the feelings for this person that surface in you with the awareness of this possibility. Open to the levels of caring and connection it reveals in you.[11]

A number of engaged Buddhist activities draw upon familiar Western forms of social involvement and protest: mobilizing voters, writing letters to newspapers and public officials, volunteer charity work, tax resistance, and boycotts of certain products and services. For several years a group in the Berkeley area has sponsored a large number of needy families in Vietnam, regularly sending parcels of food, medicine, and clothing. The Sino-American Buddhist Association helps to resettle Southeast Asian refugees, and the Jodo Shin Buddhist Churches of America administers a Cambodian relief fund. In Asia, voluntary homelessness was once an essential attribute of a Buddhist monk; in America, involuntary homelessness may become a natural area of Buddhist engagement. The Zen Community of New York received $2.5 million from New York State in support of programs that have made housing, jobs, childcare, and job training available to formerly homeless families and other local residents.

In a parallel development on the West Coast, a Buddhist hospice in Richmond, California was awarded $47,000 by a state agency to continue its work with AIDS patients. The hospice's founder, Rev. Suhita Dharma, explained his approach:

> We try to create an extended family environment and offer a lot of compassion and loving-kindness. Most of the people who come here are not Buddhists; I don't ask them, "Are you Buddhist?" or "Are you gay?" We don't consider this to be a gay problem, and I don't try to convert them to

Buddhism, but I teach them *mettā* [loving-kindness] meditation because I have found that it helps them to deal with their pain, both physical and psychological. We try to help them come to grips with their problems so they can live and die at peace.[12]

Other activities with a distinctive Buddhistic coloration include pilgrimages, public chanting, circumambulation, construction of peace pagodas, meditation vigils at military sites and government facilities, and establishment of meditation groups in prisons. In one twelve-month period, a Colorado chapter of the Buddhist Peace Fellowship conducted a "despair-and-empowerment" workshop for forty people, held a poetry reading, organized a dance called "Give Peace a Dance," sold T-shirts and greeting cards with the slogan "Visualize World Peace," and hosted a ten-day visit by Thich Nhat Hanh.

Though few Western Buddhists have resorted to civil disobedience, that tactic was added to the list of practices in 1984 when Jim Perkins and others damaged some components of a Pershing II missile. Perkins gave further details in the following account:

> On April 22, 1984, I was one of eight people who, early in the morning before sunrise, cut through a chain link fence and carried hammers and nursing bottles full of blood we had drawn from our own bodies into the facilities of Martin-Marietta Aerospace in Orlando, Florida. . . .
>
> We spilt the blood on the missile parts and also on invoices, inventories, and other drearily ordinary papers that facilitate the preparation of holocaust. We left a declaration of intent, photographs of our children and loved ones, other symbols, and a legal document indicting the U.S. government and Martin-Marietta for . . . violation of the U.N. Charter and numerous treaties in international law.
>
> Having left a vivid and, we hoped, unambiguous statement of our intent, and having done some small but actual damage to a first-strike-capable nuclear missile, we laid down our hammers, went outside to a highly visible spot . . . to sit in a circle, hands joined to sing and pray and still our rapidly beating hearts, waiting to be found.[13]

Perkins's trial resulted in a conviction for "conspiracy" and other charges, and he was imprisoned for eighteen months. He now directs the Traprock Peace Center in Deerfield, Massachusetts.

The Teachings of Thich Nhat Hanh

Among the figures who have enhanced the prospects of a newly engaged Buddhism, one of the most influential is Thich Nhat Hanh. (Thich is the surname taken by all Vietnamese monks, and Nhat Hanh means "one action." The pronunciation is *tick-not-hahn*.) Born in 1926, Nhat Hanh entered a monastery at the age of sixteen. In the 1950s he opened the first Buddhist high school in Vietnam and helped found Van Hanh Buddhist University in Saigon. A prolific writer since his youth, he has published essays, stories, and poems in Vietnamese, French, and English. His 1963 book *Engaged Buddhism* marked the first use of that term. During the Vietnam War, Nhat Hanh led a nonpartisan Buddhist movement that sought a peaceful end to the conflict. His activities were opposed by Saigon and Hanoi alike, and thousands of his companions were shot or imprisoned as they struggled amidst the fighting to rebuild villages and resettle refugees.

In 1966 Nhat Hanh accepted a series of speaking engagements in the United States and Europe, where he provided a rare firsthand account of the torments and aspirations of the Vietnamese. Besides Dr. King, he met Secretary of Defense Robert McNamara, Pope Paul VI, members of Congress, U.N. officials, and Thomas Merton, who concluded: "He and I see things in exactly the same way."[14] Nhat Hanh then learned that he would not be allowed to return to Vietnam. He received asylum in France and became chairman of the Buddhist delegation to the Paris peace talks. Still in exile, he now resides in Plum Village, France—meditating, gardening, writing, leading retreats, and coordinating international relief efforts for refugees and children. Nhat Hanh's calm and deeply penetrating manner prompted an American Zen teacher to call him "a cross between a cloud, a snail, and a piece of heavy machinery—a true religious presence."[15]

For Thich Nhat Hanh, engaged Buddhism encompasses meditation, mindfulness in daily life, involvement in one's family, and political responsiveness. At times he even dismisses the term he coined as a misnomer: "Engaged Buddhism is just Buddhism. If you practice Buddhism in your family, in society, it is engaged Buddhism."[16] Increasingly, Nhat Hanh focuses on a family-oriented practice that is intended to be easily accessible to Westerners ("family" is liberally defined). He writes:

> We talk about social service, service to humanity, service for others who are far away, helping to bring peace to the world—but we often forget that it is the very people around us that we must live for first of all. If you cannot serve your wife or husband or child or parent—how are you going to serve society?[17]

In 1989 Nhat Hanh conducted a four-day retreat in California for fifty-six young people, from toddlers to teenagers (accompanied by fifty adults). Among the practices he introduced was "hugging meditation"—participants were instructed to hug a loved one, breathe consciously, and contemplate the preciousness of the person in their arms. In a similar spirit, Nhat Hanh advocates smiling as a "basic form of peace work," because even a single smile contributes in a real way to another person's well-being.[18]

Westerners attracted to Buddhism have been looking for ways to actualize its tenets in a culture that lacks a strong commitment to monasticism. Nhat Hanh presents a style of teaching and practice that might be described as spirituality democratic: students are urged to practice as best they can on their own; they are not asked to make a personal commitment to a master; and they are welcome to maintain prior affiliations with other religious groups (including Buddhist ones). Nhat Hanh's vision of a family-oriented practice may yield a new synthesis of Buddhist spirituality and actual social conditions. Or it may be unrealistic, especially in a non-Buddhist culture, to expect families to provide much of the support and guidance that larger religious communities have traditionally offered.

For Nhat Hanh, the one sure source of a peaceful family and a peaceful world is a peaceful mind. At the heart of his teachings is a conviction that peacework is more of an inner activity than an outer one: "It is not by going out for a demonstration against nuclear missiles that we can bring about peace. It is with our capacity of smiling, breathing, and being peace that we can make peace."[19] Nhat Hanh further claims that personal peace is immediately accessible if one knows where to look; he tells readers and listeners to "touch" the peace and joy that is already within them. First, some common mental habits must be recognized and stopped:

> It is ridiculous to say, "Wait until I finish this, then I will be free to live in peace." What is "this"? A diploma, a job, a house, the payment of a debt? If you think that way, peace may never come. There is always another "this" that will follow the present one. If you are not living in peace at this moment, you will never be able to.[20]

Several of Nhat Hanh's books about meditation include little or no reference to political peacework or other forms of social engagement. When he considers meditation broadly, he writes that it is not an escape from suffering or a withdrawal from society. On the contrary, meditation prepares one for "reentry into society" and helps one "stay in society." Like countless Buddhists, Nhat Hanh values the breath as an indispensable tool for calming the body, focusing the mind, and clarifying awareness. "Breathing is a means of awakening and maintaining full attention in order to . . . see the nature of all things," he asserts. The method he prefers is focused awareness: "Breathing in, I am aware that I am breathing in. Breathing out, I am aware that I am breathing out."[21] Because modern people rarely live in monasteries or forest retreats, Nhat Hanh urges them to maintain awareness of the breath throughout their daily activities. He has created numerous poems and guided meditations that can be used as accompaniments to the breath. For example, the following is meant to be recited (mentally) in two full breaths:

> Breathing in, I calm my body.
> Breathing out, I smile.
> Dwelling in the present moment,
> I know this is a wonderful moment![22]

Nhat Hanh also emphasizes walking meditation. His instructions are straightforward:

> Choose a nice road for your practice, along the shore of a river, in a park, on the flat roof of a building, in the woods, or along a bamboo fence. Such places are ideal, but they are not essential. I know there are people who practice walking meditation in reformation camps, even in small prison cells. . . .
> Slow down and concentrate on your steps. Be aware of each move. Walk straight ahead with dignity, calm, and comfort. Consciously make an imprint on the ground as you step. Walk as the Buddha would.[23]

Characteristically, Nhat Hanh links this practice to the state of the world, saying, "If your steps are peaceful, the world will have peace."[24]

Meditating, breathing, and walking are variant forms of mindfulness, a practice common to most schools of Buddhism. Nhat Hanh's followers attempt to set aside a regular "day of mindfulness," a kind of Buddhist Sabbath that can be observed individually or with a group. On this day one wakes up alertly, begins to follow the breath even before getting out of bed, bathes in a conscious and leisurely manner, performs only necessary tasks, engages in quiet periods of seated and walking meditation, and so on. Families with young children are encouraged to use the day to be together, rest, play, and nourish themselves in the same spirit of mindfulness. Circumstances permitting, Nhat Hanh suggests that all movements be done at reduced speed:

> Whatever the tasks, do them slowly and with ease, in mindfulness. Don't do any task in order to get it over with. Resolve to do each job in a relaxed way, with all your attention. Enjoy and be one with your work.[25]

Nhat Hanh continues to develop new methods to aid contemporary Western students in their practice of mindfulness. The ringing of a telephone, for example, can be used as a signal to recollect the breath. Rather than leaping anxiously to quell a jarring intrusion, one breathes calmly and consciously for three full rings. "How lucky for the person on the other end!" adds Nhat Hanh, who teaches such techniques to children as well as adults.

In 1964, while still in Vietnam, Nhat Hanh founded a Buddhist community of activist-practitioners known as the Tiep Hien Order. As he later wrote, "The aim of Tiep Hien is to study, experiment, and apply Buddhism in an intelligent and effective way to modern life, both individual and societal."[26] The original Vietnamese community did not survive the Communist takeover, but a group called the Order of Interbeing has become its successor in the West. The most committed adherents serve an apprenticeship of one to five years before ordination, and each year they are expected to spend a certain number of weeks in retreat. Ordained and lay members strive to uphold the first five precepts of Buddhism (no killing, stealing, sexual misconduct, lying, or taking of intoxicants) plus a related set of fourteen precepts. The supplementary precepts can be summarized as follows:

1. Do not be idolatrous about or bound to any doctrine, theory, or ideology, even a Buddhist one.
2. Do not think the knowledge you presently possess is changeless absolute truth.
3. Do not force others to adopt your views, whether by authority, threat, money, propaganda, or even education.
4. Do not avoid contact with suffering or close your eyes to suffering.
5. Do not accumulate wealth while millions remain hungry.
6. Do not maintain anger or hatred.
7. Do not lose yourself in distraction, inwardly or outwardly.
8. Do not utter words that can create discord or cause your community to split apart.
9. Do not say untruthful things for the sake of personal advantage or to impress people.
10. Do not use the Buddhist community for personal gain or profit, or transform your community into a political party.
11. Do not live with a vocation that is harmful to humans or nature.
12. Do not kill. Do not let others kill.
13. Possess nothing that should belong to others.
14. Do not mistreat your body.[27]

These precepts are administered in a tolerant manner, because it is recognized that even the best-intentioned people cannot adhere to them absolutely. A single footstep, for example, may kill many beings too small to see. So "even the Buddha, while he was walking and drinking and eating, could not be entirely nonviolent."[28] The point is to uphold the spirit of each precept as faithfully as possible.

Like other contemporary Buddhist activists, Nhat Hanh elicits critical responses from certain quarters. Buddhist practitioners who give precedence to prolonged meditation suspect that Nhat Hanh overemphasizes mindfulness at the expense of deep self-realization. In contrast, those who give priority to the resolution of urgent social problems tend to regard Nhat Hanh's teachings as too contemplative or simplistic. How many people, they ask, will be persuaded that smiling or hugging have a significant impact on the world? Are hungry refugees expected to enjoy inner peace regardless of their external circumstances? Nhat Hanh may also invite criticism as a political strategist. He readily acknowledges the failures of his peace movement in Vietnam, though he points out that his "lonely" band of volunteers was pitted against the two most powerful nations in the world. "I suffered a lot from the war," he once confided. "When five of my workers were assassinated by the bank of a river, someone told me I was the commander of a nonviolent army and I had to be prepared to take losses. But how could I not cry?" Looking back, Nhat Hanh concludes that the odds against success were overwhelming: "I see that the nonviolent struggle for peace in Vietnam was a beautiful one. It did not succeed very much, not because it was wrong, but because it did not have all the conditions it needed."[29]

In 1977 Nhat Hanh was thwarted in a well-intentioned attempt to rescue hundreds of boat people in the Gulf of Siam. His plan was to ship them secretly to Guam or Australia, but an untimely leak to the press alerted local governments, and the boat people were instead consigned to refugee camps in Malaysia. In response to this setback, Nhat Hanh went into partial retreat for five years. Discussing the Gulf of Siam incident in a 1990 interview, he still seemed troubled by the apparent disjunction between the spiritual integrity of his group and the political results of their action:

It was very painful. Yet, we had conducted the operation in meditation. We lived, I can say, like holy people. . . . If we were not mindful, people could die. We sat [in meditation] late into the night every night, reciting the *Heart Sutra* after the sitting, and we lived as though in a monastery. So I am still very content and pleased with the operation, but the conditions were not right.[30]

Whatever its practical or theoretical limitations, Nhat Hanh's model of engaged Buddhism seeks to achieve a constructive balance between inner work and concern for others. In his vision, spiritual practice and political activism are mutually reinforcing, not mutually exclusive. Even in the face of the terrible violence he has encountered, Nhat Hanh continues to believe that inner peace is possible amidst the most hellish conditions. Alluding to the boat people, he asserts that in an overcrowded boat adrift on a turbulent sea, if there is just one person who remains inwardly calm, everyone benefits immeasurably. Nhat Hanh himself seems to exemplify just such a person. Like the Dalai Lama, he serves as a beacon for thousands of contemporary Buddhists around the world.

The Buddhist Peace Fellowship

Engaged Buddhism is a loosely coordinated movement, nationally and internationally. The groups that appear (and disappear) include offshoots of established congregations, committees concerned with a particular issue, campaigns on behalf of prisoners or refugees, makeshift schools for nonviolence training, fact-finding missions to foreign countries, and so on. While these ever-shifting groups may be peripherally aware of each other, networking and cooperation is sporadic. In North America, the one organization that provides an umbrella for most forms of Buddhist engagement is the Buddhist Peace Fellowship (BPF). On a wider stage, the recently created International Network of Engaged Buddhists (INEB) has attempted to promote various causes, especially in regard to the predominantly Buddhist countries of Asia.

Since its inception in 1978 (on Robert Aitken's porch in Maui), the BPF has grown at a modest but steady rate. The contributions of its two thousand members support a small office in Berkeley, one national coordinator, and a quarterly journal. Recent projects have included conflict mediation, nonviolent eco-activist training, the preparation of Buddhist response packets on issues of national concern, a summer institute for the practice of engaged Buddhism, delegations to troubled areas of the world, and increased Buddhist representation at conferences on peace and the environment. Local chapters have been formed in about twenty-five U.S. cities and towns. Some of these groups generate schedules full of varied activities, while others serve primarily as vehicles of mutual support and sharing. In practice, a member who proposes a local or national project must also be willing to assume responsibility for its implementation.

No single leader has emerged to stamp his or her own vision on the evolution of the Buddhist Peace Fellowship. In true grassroots fashion, power is decentralized and initiative comes from the local level. Though many members turn first to Thich Nhat Hanh for inspiration and guidance, others favor a different Buddhist tradition or a different style of social activism. At this early stage, the BPF has not yet been able to formulate a well-defined image or message that might attract a broader constituency; its profile is so low that it is not even known within the American peace movement. As a point of contrast, one could cite the Plowshares campaign conceived by Christian peace activists. Increasingly visible in the past decade, the Plowshares group has a simple slogan ("Swords into Plowshares"), a straightforward message (nuclear weapons violate a higher law), a clear-cut target (U.S. military sites), and a distinctive method (civil disobedience). A comparison between the BPF and a mainstream religious organizaion is revealing in a different way. For instance, when the bishops of the United Methodist Church issued their antinuclear pastoral letter in 1986, they had access to 9.4 million constituents, including seventy-nine members of Congress.

The Buddhist Peace Fellowship appeals to Westerners who have embraced Buddhism and who also believe that their chosen path must address the pressing issues of the day. More a religious movement than a political one, the BPF is fueled by an expressed need to modify or extend traditional spiritual practice. Whereas most Asian Buddhists who become active in social affairs do so because they or their communities are politically endangered, few Western Buddhists feel threatened in that way. If engaged Buddhists in the First World sometimes seem to be talking mostly to themselves or looking around for direction, it may be due to a lack of direct exposure to suffering, especially in international contexts. The transmission of Buddhism to the West repeats a familiar pattern, in which it is first taken up by the more privileged sectors of society. Buddhism's new Western adherents are predominantly white and well-educated, from middle class and upper middle class backgrounds. Aspiring Buddhist activists who enjoy such advantages have discovered that concern for others, however sincere, can mysteriously resist translation into action. Yet those who do find a way to work with homeless mothers, or dying AIDS patients, or Cambodian refugees report that personal participation is as liberating for the "helper" as for the "helped."

International Dimensions of Engaged Buddhism

Socially engaged Buddhism acquires a different cast in Asian and Third World countries. When Buddhists are persecuted by dictatorial regimes or by non-Buddhist ethnic majorities, "engagement" takes the form of a life-and-death struggle for political or cultural survival. Those involved in such conflicts typically have little interest in the theoretical implications of nonviolence or the latest innovations in spiritual/activist practice. Some reluctantly conclude, "We see no way to defend ourselves but to fight back."[31] Just as the meaning of engagement differs in Western and Asian contexts, so does the meaning of Buddhism. When one is born and raised in a Buddhist milieu, Buddhism can be a cultural and national identity as much as a religious one. In some cases, activists avow little or no reliance on traditional forms of practice; in other cases, Buddhism doubles as an expedient vehicle for pursuing social or political leverage.

Many of the predominantly or formerly Buddhist countries of Asia are embroiled in economic, military, and ecological crises. In Chinese-occupied Tibet, Buddhists are suffering the systematic destruction of their religious/cultural heritage and the devastation of their land's natural resources. When small groups of monks and nuns have attempted peaceful protest marches, they have been shot down or beaten to death by Chinese troops.[32] The only forms of engagement currently available to the Tibetans are diplomacy and publicity, but efforts to exert international pressure on the Beijing government have so far been ineffectual. In Cambodia, where a million people are believed to have died during Khmer Rouge rule (1975–79), decades of civil war have left the country prostrate. The once-thriving Cambodian Sangha has been almost totally eradicated; education of Cambodian novice-monks in Thai refugee camps depends upon materials donated by Buddhists in other countries.

Burma, formerly the "rice bowl of Asia," is now one of the poorest nations in the world. Since 1962 it has been ruled by a brutal and xenophobic military dictatorship. During the summer of 1988, students and Buddhist monks led a popular uprising that briefly challenged the state, but the euphoria ended when soldiers began firing at random into unarmed crowds and nearby buildings. In Rangoon nearly a thousand people were killed in three days. Though Burma remains a devoutly Buddhist country, monasteries were also raided. An American eyewitness reported:

> They started grabbing people, particularly monks. They humiliated the monks by kicking them and making them take down barricades. They marched into monasteries and pagodas with their boots on, carrying weapons. The abbot of one monastery confronted the soldiers at the entrance and told them, "If you want to come into my monastery, you have to shoot me first." Finally, he reached an agreement with them: they could enter if they took their boots off and left their weapons outside. By that time the student demonstrators inside had been spirited out.[33]

In September 1990 the Buddhist clergy initiated a widespread "religious boycott" of soldiers and their families, a significant act of civil disobedience. As this writing the Burmese military regime continues to detain and abuse thousands of political prisoners; among them is Aung San Suu Kyi, leader of the National League for Democracy and winner of the 1991 Nobel Peace Prize.

Sadly, the litany of suppression and suffering goes on. The minority Buddhist hill tribes of Bangladesh are ruthlessly persecuted by the majority Muslims. In Vietnam, distinguished Buddhist monks who dare to criticize the government are jailed without trial. In Nepal, the Hindu majority accords second-class status to the sizeable Buddhist minority, almost forty percent of the population. As Nepal struggles to shift to a constitutional system, the future role of Buddhists remains uncertain. For nearly a decade, Sri Lanka has been rent by civil strife between the Hindu Tamils and the Sinhalese Buddhists, with the Sangha itself split into rival factions. Though Buddhists are a majority within Sri Lanka, they feel threatened by the populous Hindus in nearby India. In mainland China, Buddhism has been rejected as a feudal anachronism by the Communists. The few active temples that survive are administered by the state, and most Chinese young people know nothing of their country's rich Buddhist heritage.

Buddhism is more privileged in Thailand and Japan, and those countries accordingly reveal distinctive forms of Buddhist engagement. In relatively prosperous Thailand, the monarchy and the Sangha have traditionally supported each other. On the national level, respected monks such as Buddhadasa were able to exert significant influence; on the local level, some of the more engaged monks and laypeople managed to establish communal rice banks, preserve endangered forests, and open schools for nonviolence training. However, generals who seized power in February 1991 have harassed several outspoken Buddhist leaders, and the political climate in Thailand is not stable.

Japan's situation is anomalous in several respects. Most Japanese are nominally Buddhist, though modernization and secularization have undermined the vitality of traditional religion. Although Japan is an Asian nation, it has also become a First World one, and it shows little restraint in taking advantage of the natural resources, labor, and markets of its less developed Asian neighbors, Buddhist or not. Socially engaged Buddhists in Japan remain marginal in Buddhist circles and in society at large, yet they are quietly active in various way. Some have taken up issues such as nuclear proliferation, domestic prostitution, and discrimination against minorities; others volunteer in hospitals and examine biomedical issues from a spiritual perspective. Awareness of global issues has been slow to develop, though some of the newer sects campaign for peace internationally. In 1979 a major branch of Zen spawned the Japan Sotoshu Relief Committee, which has successfully channeled aid to families in Bangkok slums and refugees in Thai border camps.[34]

The International Network of Engaged Buddhists (INEB) was inaugurated in February 1989 at a meeting in Uthaitani, Thailand. A part-time staff of four, working out of a one-room office in Bangkok, coordinates ongoing projects and publishes a journal three times a year. The moving force behind the new organization is Sulak Sivaraksa, one of the contributors to the present volume. Born into a cultured Thai family and educated at a university in Wales, Sivaraksa has been an influential (and often controversial) critic of Thai society since the early 1960s. In recent years he has organized missions to mediate the internal strife in Sri Lanka, worked to set up "jungle universities" for Burmese students in refugees camps, and made several speaking tours to North America and Japan. Undaunted by personal risk, Sivaraksa has repeatedly called for democratic reform in Thailand. In 1984 he was arrested for an alleged affront to the king, but the charge was soon withdrawn. In September 1991, after Sivaraksa gave a pro-democracy speech at a university, the new military junta issued another warrant for his arrest. He took refuge in the German embassy in Bangkok, then secretly fled the country. During his involuntary exile, Sivaraksa has been working to increase international awareness of Thailand's democracy movement.

The first conference of the International Network of Engaged Buddhists brought together thirty-six people from eleven countries. In 1990 the second annual meeting attracted over fifty people from sixteen nations, including a senior Cambodian monk, a Vietnamese professor from Hanoi, the editor of a Mongolian Buddhist journal, four Burmese students from a refugee camp, a representative of a new Buddhist movement in India, an American-born Theravada teacher active in England, a bearded Buryat monk from the former U.S.S.R., numerous Thai monks, a Welshman, a French woman, several Americans, five Japanese priests, and two multilingual Japanese interpreters. The 1991 session drew ninety delegates with a comparable range of backgrounds.

Participants in these first annual conferences divided themselves into working subgroups that addressed topics such as education, human rights, women's issues, nonviolence, and "spirituality and activism." A number of theoretical issues were initially offered for consideration, including the following: What makes "engaged Buddhism" Buddhist? Does it go beyond doing good? How does "engagement" differ from "attachment"? Can social activism be genuine spiritual practice, and if so, how? How can the basic teachings of Buddhism be expressed meaningfully to the materially poor, physically oppressed, and educationally deprived? Actual group discussions tended to focus on specific problems rather than abstract principles, because most of the participants were primarily concerned about current social or political crises in their own countries.

A gathering as diverse as an INEB conference must contend with many obstacles that result from the mix of cultures, languages, religious sensibilities, styles of leadership, and priorities. For instance, the orange-robed Theravada monks were seated on a platform above the other attendees, as is the custom in Thailand. After a Japanese priest (clad in T-shirt and pants) politely objected to this arrangement, the Thai monks agreed to sit on the same level as the others in attendance. At certain points the

Third World/Asian members of oppressed Buddhist groups seemed to have little in common with the First World/Western members of privileged Buddhist groups. Some of the Asians wondered if the Westerners were studying the event rather than participating in it, and they were bemused by Westerners' requests for more emphasis on meditation. In contrast, some of Westerners wondered if there was anything Buddhist about the political passions of the Asians, and they were alarmed by the lack of ecological awareness among the Third World representatives.

Cherished views get challenged repeatedly in such gatherings. For example, an American whose advocacy of nonviolence remains untested may be drawn into conversation with a Burmese student who associates nonviolence with impotence, having seen his companions gunned down in the city and ambushed in the jungle. Similar encounters have prompted Joanna Macy to comment:

> Many of us feel it is inappropriate to pass judgment on the use of arms and violence against those who are invading, killing, blockading, and destroying. For us as members of this Empire to sit by and say, "Oh, but the response should be nonviolent, and it is wrong to take up arms...." Well, I simply cannot bring myself to do that.... I think this is an issue for a lot of people who want to be serious about nonviolence.[35]

No single formula can be expected to resolve all situations, but the dialogue itself seems to yield benefits for those involved. Westerners tend to become more humble and flexible concerning the application of nonviolent principles to actual situations, while Asians are often able to gather new information about nonviolent methods that have been effective in other dangerous circumstances.

There have been turning points in Buddhism's past history when people believed that they lived in an age of religious degeneration and potential worldwide disaster. Often during such periods the usual sources of religious inspiration were no longer persuasive, and the chances of personal salvation seemed slim. And yet these were also some of the most creative eras in Buddhism's development. Today, many Buddhists are once against struggling to reestablish meaningful foundations for the spiritual striving of individuals and the harmonious functioning of society. An important new element in the mix is international and planetary awareness. Whereas Buddhism was once identified only with particular cultures, the modern world allows for a shared understanding of Buddhism that bridges cultural variations without denying them. Some form of social engagement will undoubtedly be an accepted component of a globally oriented Buddhism, though the expressions of that engagement will continue to vary.

Notes

1. Thich Nhat Hanh, *Vietnam: Lotus in a Sea of Fire* (New York: Hill and Wang, 1967), 107.
2. Catherine Ingram, *In the Footsteps of Gandhi: Conversations with Spiritual Social Activists* (Berkeley: Parallax Press, 1990), 87, 78.
3. Jim Perkins, "Civil Disobedience," *Buddhist Peace Fellowship Newsletter* 8:1–2 (Spring 1986), 5.
4. Ingram, *In the Footsteps of Gandhi*, 161.
5. Nelson Foster, "To Enter the Marketplace," in Fred Eppsteiner, ed., *The Path of Compassion: Writings on Socially Engaged Buddhism*, rev. ed. (Berkeley: Parallax Press, 1988), 49.
6. Robert A. F. Thurman, "Nagarjuna's Guidelines for Buddhist Social Action," in Eppsteiner, *The Path of Compassion*, 129.
7. Christopher Titmuss, "Interactivity: Sitting for Peace and Standing for Parliament," in Eppsteiner, *The Path of Compassion*, 184.
8. *Middlebury* magazine (Autumn 1984), 34.
9. Maruyama Teruo, et al., "*Bukkyō no genzai*," in *Bukkyō* 9 (October 1989), 104.
10. Thich Nhat Hanh's many books include *Zen Keys* (1974), *The Miracle of Mindfulness!* (1975), *Being Peace* (1987), *Peace is Every Step* (1991), and others cited in these pages. The Dalai Lama's lectures and teachings are regularly compiled in such works as *Kindness, Clarity, and Insight* (1984) and *Ocean of Wisdom: Guidelines for Living* (1990). *Shambhala: The Sacred Path of the Warrior* (1984), by the late Tibetan teacher Chogyam Trungpa, examines "the meaning of an enlightened society and how it can be realized." Robert Aitken contemplates Zen Buddhist ethics in *The Mind of Clover* (1984). *Ambedkar and Buddhism* (1986), by Sangharakshita, assesses the recent Buddhist social movement in India. Joanna Macy's *Despair and Personal Power in the Nuclear Age* (1983) offers Buddhist-inspired techniques for responding to global crises; her most recent collection of essays is *World as Lover, World as Self* (1991). The first anthology of contemporary writings on engaged Buddhism is *The Path of Compassion*, originally issued in 1985 and updated in 1988. *The Social Face of Buddhism* (1990), by Ken Jones, expands upon his seminal pamphlet "Buddhism and Social Action" (1981). Christopher Titmuss's *Spirit for Change* (1989) and Catherine Ingram's *In the Footsteps of Gandhi* (1990) record interviews with contemporary spiritual activists.
11. Joanna Macy, *Despair and Personal Power in the Nuclear Age* (Philadelphia: New Society Publishers, 1983), 155.
12. "Ven. Suhita's Buddhist AIDS Hospice," *BPF Newsletter* 11:2 (Summer 1989), 5.

13. Perkins, "Civil Disobedience," *BPF Newsletter* 8:1–2 (Spring 1986), 4.
14. Thich Nhat Hanh, *Being Peace* (Berkeley: Parallax Press, 1987), back cover.
15. Richard Baker, in Nhat Hanh, *Being Peace*, viii.
16. Arnold Kotler, "Breathing and Smiling: Traveling with Thich Nhat Hanh," *BPF Newsletter* 11:2 (Summer 1989), 22.
17. Thich Nhat Hanh, *The Miracle of Mindfulness!* (Boston: Beacon Press, 1975), 75.
18. Nhat Hanh, *Being Peace*, 5.
19. Ibid., 9.
20. Thich Nhat Hanh, *The Sun My Heart* (Berkeley: Parallax Press, 1988), 125.
21. Nhat Hanh, *Being Peace*, 45; Thich Nhat Hanh, *The Sutra on the Full Awareness of Breathing* (Berkeley: Parallax Press, 1988), 22; Lee Clinger Lesser, "Retreat for Young People," *BPF Newsletter* 11:2 (Summer 1989), 24.
22. Thich Nhat Hanh, *Present Moment Wonderful Moment: Mindfulness Verses for Daily Living* (Berkeley: Parallax Press, 1990), 32.
23. Thich Nhat Hanh, *A Guide to Walking Meditation* (Nyack, N.Y.: Fellowship of Reconciliation, 1985), 15.
24. Ibid., 15.
25. Nhat Hanh, *The Miracle of Mindfulness!*, 29.
26. Thich Nhat Hanh, *Interbeing: Commentaries on the Tiep Hien Precepts* (Berkeley: Parallax Press, 1987), 16.
27. Excerpted from Nhat Hanh, *Interbeing*, 27–57.
28. Ingram, *In the Footsteps of Gandhi*, 87–88.
29. Katy Butler, "Vietnam Vets Retreat," *BPF Newsletter* 11:2 (Summer 1989), 29; Ingram, *In the Footsteps of Gandhi*, 89.
30. Ingram, *In the Footsteps of Gandhi*, 90.
31. All Burma Students' Democratic Front, *Dawn* 1:9 (May 1989), 1.
32. See, for example, Canyon Sam, "Woman Shot in Tibet," *BPF Newsletter* (Fall 1989), 14–15.
33. Stan Sesser, "A Rich Country Gone Wrong," *The New Yorker* (9 October 1989), 88–89.
34. Kenneth Kraft, "*Gendai Nihon ni okeru Bukkyō to shakai katsudō*," *Daikai* 27 (November/December 1990), 20–23; *Daikai* 28 (January 1991), 59–64.
35. Ingram, *In the Footsteps of Gandhi*, 155.

2

Nonviolence and the Self in Early Buddhism

by Luis O. Gómez

In Buddhism, the principle of nonviolence (*ahiṃsā*) projects an ideal of universal peace, which can be expanded to include the notion of a peaceful mind. The logic of Buddhist doctrine in fact places the mind first: religious striving for cosmic order and harmony takes place in the mind. In most Western traditions, the mind is part of the world, and there is a moral imperative to preserve that world. Early Buddhists saw it differently: the world is preserved in the mind, and the imperative is for mental cultivation. Accordingly, the ancient function of ritual—creating, reestablishing, or maintaining order—is taken over by meditation and self-cultivation. This orientation can be called ecology of mind, in the sense that the total environment of the human being is encapsulated in the mental world.[1] The Buddhist ideal of universal harmony not only includes the mind, it establishes a synonymity between mind and cosmos.

At the same time, proponents of *ahiṃsā* often show a tendency, subtle or expressed, to justify nonviolence through self-righteousness. In other words, there is latent in any credo of nonviolence an assertion of self, a separation of self from others, and a hierarchy of virtue. Abstaining from certain patterns of behavior is considered the basis of a socially acceptable person and a prerequisite of morality. Although nonviolent behavior may be associated with self-effacement and compassionate thoughts, it embraces certain features of the self and excludes others, thereby serving as a

31

powerful tool of self-definition. This dynamic can operate on a group level as well, clarifying the identity of a Buddhist community.

These are not the only interpretations of *ahiṃsā* generated by the Pali scriptures and related Buddhist texts. Elsewhere in the early literature, seminal legends extol an abstention from violence that is so uncompromising it embraces self-sacrifice. Certain other sources, such as the vows taken by monks and lay devotees, disclose the ritualistic dimensions of nonviolent behavior. Additional approaches are found in the edicts of the Buddhist king Aśoka (third century B.C.E.), reflecting a ruler's concern for social harmony. Depending on the context, the foundation or foundational value of nonviolence may be compassion, moral purity, the inherent worth of living beings, or the realization of no-self. Not all of these perspectives are necessarily consistent, yet they have remained relevant throughout the history of Buddhism. In many cases they can be universalized and applied to contemporary discussions among Buddhists and non-Buddhists alike.

Two Jātaka Tales

Much of the lore of Indian Buddhism is preserved in the *Jātaka*s, stories of the Buddha's compassion and heroism in his previous incarnations, whether in human or animal form. In these colorful accounts, the Bodhisattva (on his way to becoming the Buddha) repeatedly gives up his own life for other living beings. His sacrifices are customarily understood as expressions of "selflessness." Buddhism values selflessness in at least two of the meanings accepted by Westerners: detachment from self, and recognition of the value of another's life, which may even exceed the value of one's own life. In the abstract, therefore, the message of these legends of self-sacrifice seems uplifting. The concrete images used to develop the motif, however, lend themselves to interpretations of selflessness with which the modern reader may not always feel at ease.

We read, for instance, of the Buddha's exemplary nonviolent behavior in the story of his earlier incarnation as an ascetic named Speaker of Patience (Kṣāntivādin). A cruel king falsely accused Speaker of Patience of seducing the king's wives. Though the ascetic initially spoke in his own defense, his rejoinder was to no avail. Realizing that the king was obsessed by jealousy and blinded by anger, the accused man "kept silent, feeling pity for the king, who was like a patient refusing a physician's advice." The king then drew his sword and began to cut Speaker of Patience into pieces, yet the ascetic did not complain or make any further effort to defend himself. "Even as he saw his limbs being cut off, the ascetic felt no pain, because he had made a habit of friendliness [to living beings]; rather, when he saw that the king had fallen from virtue, he grieved for him."[2] The behavior of Speaker of Patience embodies a type of nonviolence that might be described as the selfless *acceptance* of violence. But most of us probably have mixed feelings about this example and the ideal it represents. Why did the ascetic not make more of an effort to defend himself, using nonviolent or perhaps even violent means if necessary?

Total surrender is also the motif of another *Jātaka* story in which the Buddha, in a previous lifetime as a prince, sacrifices himself for a hungry tigress and her cubs. The starving tigress was about to devour her own cubs in order to sate her hunger. Encountering this scene, the prince felt compassion not only for the cubs but also for the tigress, a symbol of the evil that is caused by delusion and despair. Standing at the edge of a cliff, he resolved: "I will throw my body over the precipice, to protect the tigress from killing her young, and to protect the cubs from their mother." He then leapt to his death to be devoured by the tigress.[3]

The Bodhisattva's sacrifice, although intended as an act of virtue, may seem unnatural, if not bizarre. When the ideal of nonviolence is carried to such an extreme, it strikes us as unrealistic. In the West we accept the idea of sacrificing ourselves for others in some kind of heroic manner, but the immediate cause and agent of a "supreme" sacrifice is usually external to the self. The notion of actively causing one's own death to save another, especially an animal, would probably be regarded by most Westerners as an exaggeration of the virtue of selflessness.

However contrived these two *Jātaka* tales may seem, they are paradigmatic expressions of the Buddhist ideal of *ahiṃsā*. One may distinguish in these legends at least two facets of the virtue of nonviolence: actively removing the causes of harm to others, and abstaining from hurting others even when it involves accepting harm to oneself. The prince in the story of the tigress practices nonviolence by actively mitigating the harm the tigress and her cubs would otherwise suffer, whereas Speaker of Patience passively accepts harm to himself rather than harm others. The dominant feature of the ascetic's behavior is abstention: he refrains from paying back violence with violence. Though Buddhists in many cultures have drawn inspiration from such accounts, a number of points compel further consideration. For example: Are compassionate involvement and virtuous abstention ethically equivalent? Can nonviolence be explained purely as an altruistic ideal? Is abstention motivated as much by a desire to affirm the self as by an aspiration to become free from the self?

The Edicts of King Aśoka

Some of the issues raised by these *Jātaka* stories may be clarified by looking at other Buddhist formulations or applications of nonviolence. For instance, the Indian king Aśoka tried to propagate a lofty ideal of nonviolence without recommending to his subjects that they sacrifice themselves for hungry tigresses or cruel rulers. King Aśoka's conversion to nonviolence, described in Donald Swearer's essay, was followed by a series of edicts inscribed on rocks and pillars. The First Rock Edict declared in part:

> Hundreds of thousands of living creatures were formerly slaughtered every day for curries in the kitchens of His Majesty, Beloved of the Gods, of Sweet Countenance. As this edict is being inscribed, only three living beings are killed daily: two peacocks and one deer. And the deer is not slaughtered regularly. In the future, not even these three animals will be slaughtered.[4]

This inscription has sometimes been read with cynicism, because the King shows some reluctance to give up his favorite curries. I see this passage, however, as reflecting Aśoka's characteristic candor—he does not hide his human weaknesses. The ideal of nonviolence is no different from other human ideals, and there is no reason why we should not allow for hesitation and growth in its adoption and application. Other inscriptions give further indications of the evolution of Aśoka's thought on nonviolence. The edict cited above marks the King's transition from meat-eating to vegetarianism, and it proscribes animal sacrifices in the name of religion. The Fourth Rock Edict, inscribed twelve years after Aśoka's coronation, further declares that "abstaining from the destruction of life is good."[5] Later in his reign Aśoka continued to strengthen these policies: his Fifth Pillar Edict forbids the wanton destruction of forests, and it lists selected species to be protected from butchers and hunters alike.

If we apply our own interpretive categories to these edicts, they seem to vacillate between expressions of several different values—ethical, social, ecological, and religious. For example, which of these values underlies the injunction against destroying certain species of trees? Another part of the Fifth Pillar Edict proscribes the killing of "she-goats and sows that are pregnant or are in milk, also the young less than six months."[6] What is the rationale behind that statute? This same inscription limits but does not forbid hunting, which is proscribed only on festival days or on the days of Buddhist retreat. At those times "one is not to kill or sell fish. And on those same days one is not to kill other animals that live in the elephant forest and the fisheries."[7] These regulations indicate that the King has religious or ritual values that lead him to restrict hunting and fishing, as well as conservationist values that lead him to keep preserves for certain species in the kingdom. It appears that Aśoka was motivated both by a belief in the inherent value of nonviolence and a concern for the preservation of social harmony. This orientation can also be seen in the Second Rock Edict:

Everywhere [the King] has established provisions for two kinds of medical treatment: treatment of men, and treatment of animals. Wherever the proper medicinal herbs suitable for men and animals were lacking, they have been imported and planted. Also, where roots and fruits were lacking, they have been imported and planted. Wells have been dug....[8]

King Aśoka had begun to reinterpret the doctrine of nonviolence in a broad sense that embraced social harmony. This is significant, for the Buddhist texts known to him at that time (as far as we can tell) profess a view of *ahiṃsā* that is narrower than Aśoka's understanding.[9] For instance, the two *Jātaka* tales cited above are less motivated by social goals and more focused on self-cultivation. And yet Aśoka did not reject earlier formulations. In the Seventh Pillar Edict, where Aśoka addresses the relationship between spiritual practice and moral prescriptions, we see that ultimately he too subordinated nonviolence to an ethic of self-development:

> People can be induced to advance in the Dharma by only two means, namely moral prescriptions and meditation [*bhāvanā* or spiritual cultivation]. Of the two, moral prescriptions are the lesser, meditation the greater. The moral prescriptions I have promulgated include rules making certain animals inviolable, and I have established many other rules as well. But even in the case of abstention from injuring and killing living creatures, it is by meditation that people have made the greatest progress in the Dharma.[10]

The Ritual Context of Nonviolence

In the human psyche the association between nonviolence, abstention, and purity is so close that at times it seems the only reason people want to shun violence is to avoid the taint of blood on their hands; and the only reason they want to be morally pure is to escape some vague but potent polluting influence. Many stanzas in the *Dhammapada*, for instance, describe evil as impurity that pollutes, corrupts, and harms the self. Someone who is violent stains or pollutes his own mind—the literature often compares the mind of one who harms others to a stained piece of cloth.[11]

In the story of the hungry tigress, the Bodhisattva wants to protect the cubs, but he also wants to protect the tigress from her own anger. The underlying principle is that anger, whether hidden or acted out, brings pain to the one who is angry. The hatred and violence manifested by the king who tortures Speaker of Patience is conceived as a disease that afflicts the king and not the ascetic. From this perspective, the most significant feature of harming others is the effect on the mind of the agent. For all the talk of protecting living beings, the central issue (for the Buddhist monk especially) seems to be cleansing the cloth of one's own mind, through a profound change in one's moral habits.

Studies on the origin of vegetarianism in Indian religions have shown that proscription of meat-eating grew out of primitive taboos against the spilling of blood.[12] Besides suggesting that *ahiṃsā* may have had ritual origins, these findings also highlight the social function of nonviolent practices. In the monastic context, nonviolence served to delimit the identity of the individual monk and the monastic community as a whole. Just as dietary rules have helped define numerous other religious groups, Asian Buddhists have long been associated with vegetarianism (even though they may not uphold it strictly). Indeed, dietary rules and precepts of nonviolence intermingle in the earliest Buddhist monastic code, the Vinaya.

The ideals and symbols of nonviolence have deep roots in an unconscious sphere, where purity and impurity, sacred and profane, self and other, exist in clear opposition. Accordingly, compassion and brotherhood are not sufficient explanations for the origin and spread of vegetarianism and other nonviolent practices. One must also look to myth and ritual to understand their enduring appeal. Even within Buddhism, or perhaps we should say especially in Buddhism, the ritual context remains. For example, the vows adopted at fortnightly recitations (*uposatha*) of the Buddhist moral code are expressed as follows:

> As the buddhas until the very end of their lives have abstained from killing living beings, thus will I [personal name] for the duration of one day and one night abstain from killing living beings. As the buddhas until the very end of their lives have abstained from stealing, thus will I [personal name] for the duration of one day and one night abstain from stealing. . . .[13]

Note the ritual frame: the passage does not affirm "I shall not kill any more." The vow is *only for this day*, because this is a holy day. "This is the day I really vow not to kill. This is the day when I identify myself as a Buddhist."

Such an outlook is clearly related to, and probably derived from, pan-Indian beliefs concerning the sacredness of life during particular points in the monthly cycle. This ritual frame is found in the early literature of Brahmanism and Jainism,[14] and it is also reflected in Aśokan edicts such as the following:

> Fish must not be killed or sold on the day of the full moon which begins each of the three seasons, on the Tiṣya [Sirius] full moon, on the three days which end a fortnight and begin a new one, or on fast days [a total of fifty-six days during each year].

The passage goes on to specify certain days when "bulls, he-goats, rams, boars, and other animals which are usually castrated must not be castrated."[15] Violence may not even be the principal issue in this statute. The proscription of castration has nothing to do with killing—it is a prohibition of the spilling of blood or the wasting of life-giving fluids. When the precept not to kill is treated in the same manner as injunctions against wearing perfume or dancing, the association of nonviolence with the ritual calendar becomes even more apparent. Returning to the *uposatha* vows, we find the following:

As the buddhas until the very end of their lives have abstained from wearing garlands, anointing their bodies with perfume, and wearing perfumed garments, thus will I [personal name] for the duration of one day and one night abstain from wearing garlands.... As the buddhas until the very end of their lives have abstained from participating in song and dance, playing musical instruments, and watching shows, thus will I....[16]

In the framework of these recitations of the code, abstention from harming living beings is only one of several marks of participation in the Buddhist community.

Another example of the ritual meaning of nonviolence is found in a canonical passage about monks and snakes. A monk was bitten by a poisonous snake while he was in a jungle retreat, and his companions rushed to the Buddha for advice. They lived in constant fear of these snakes, and they wished to know how they could protect themselves. So the Buddha gave them the following incantation as a protective charm:

My love to the Virupakka [snakes], my love to the Erapatha [snakes], my love to the Chabyaputta [snakes], my love to the Kanhagotama [snakes]. My love to the footless, my love to the twofooted, my love to the fourfooted, my love to the manyfooted. Let not the footless harm me, let not the twofooted harm me, let not the fourfooted harm me, let not the manyfooted harm me. All sentient beings, all breathing things, all creatures without exception, let them all see good things, may no evil befall them.[17]

In other words: So-and-so snake, I am well disposed and friendly toward you, therefore you will not bite me, therefore I am fully protected from you. In this context the expression of nonviolent intent is considered to have a protective power; the mere thought of love has the force to repel harm. Here we have a case of conscious, positive projection: if my thoughts are nonviolent, others will (or already do) feel similarly toward me. The passage reveals the close ties between danger, fear, compassion, and power over the environment.

Nonviolent intentions "protect" not only by projection, but also by restoring order. In effect, they rearrange the relative positions of different agents according to a moral framework. Thus the charm for the snakes concludes:

> The Buddha is boundless, the Dharma is boundless, the Sangha is boundless. Finite and measurable are crawlers, snakes, scorpions, centipedes, spiders, lizards, and rats. I have made a safeguard, I have made a spell. Let the creatures go away. I pay homage to the Blessed One; I pay homage to the Seven Full and Perfect Buddhas.[18]

Several features in this passage are consistent with what we have learned about ritual order from other contexts. First, a clear distinction is made between a boundless sacred order and a finite profane order that involves danger and death. Second, the believer's faith is the inherent potency of the spell is a guarantee of its efficacy. Third, the ultimate source of power for the charm is the sublime state of highly advanced beings, in this case fully enlightened buddhas.

Because "primitive" perceptions of violence reflect patterns of thought in which disorder is synonymous with pollution, the restorative force of rituals lies in their capacity to reestablish one's position in a world disturbed by moral confusion. Broadly considered, monastic regulations and the purification of one's own mind also fulfill these ritualistic functions. The instinct of self-preservation and the need for self-definition cannot easily be separated from "higher" ethical ideals, because ritual and "higher" ethics are similarly concerned with the limits of disorder. There is no reason, however, to reduce the ideal of nonviolence to an irrational mechanism. Even if *ahiṃsā* has amoral roots, its subsequent ethical interpretation is not vitiated.

Intentionality and the Valuation of Life

Although the ritualistic conception of nonviolence is as essential to early Buddhism as it is to Hinduism, preoccupation with ritual and moral purity is not the most characteristic context for nonviolence in Buddhism. While Buddhists accepted numerous pan-Indian beliefs and symbols, they also altered or rejected certain elements of their cultural heritage. In the case of nonviolence, Buddhism attempted to redefine prevailing notions of moral and ritual purity in a broader, more psychological context.

As a point of contrast, one could cite Jainism, a religion that flourished about the same time as early Indian Buddhism. The Jains proposed that evil actions, especially killing or harming living creatures, would produce bad karma. The Jains further believed in a direct connection between the action and the resulting karma, regardless of the agent's intentions. Even if one were not aware that one had caused the death of a living being—for example, by stepping on an insect while walking—evil karma would "flow into the soul," a moral burden would "accrue," and negative consequences would follow. As Christopher Chapple explains in the following chapter, Jainism had a materialistic view of moral responsibility: karma was a kind of "dust," a form of matter that would attach to the soul.[19] In other words, morality was conceived in terms of purity and impurity.

The Buddhists criticized this approach. They claimed that bad karma is "absorbed" only as a consequence of mental states pervaded by sense desire, ignorance, and wrong views about the self.[20] This position represented a shift from early, more physical notions of purity to a cognitive or psychological view of purity. The Buddhists also rejected the corresponding concept of religious merit—that by acting a certain way you gather a quantifiable mass of good or bad consequences. The Buddhist reformulation of ideal conduct is expressed in the *Dhammapada*:

> Neither wandering naked, nor [having] matted locks, nor [covering the body with] filth, dust, or ashes, nor fasting, nor sleeping on the bare ground, nor squatting for extended periods will purify a mortal who has not overcome doubts. Even if one wears the ornaments [of lay life], if one lives in peace, subdued, tame and controlled, chaste, having abandoned violence towards all living beings, then one is a true Brahman, a true ascetic, a true monk.[21]

The process by which ritual thinking was rationalized and ethicized is also seen in another version of the *uposatha* vows taken regularly by monks and lay devotees:

> All their lives Buddhist saints abandon taking life and abstain from killing. They dwell meekly and kindly, compassionate and merciful to all beings, laying aside stick and sword. During this night and day I too will abandon taking life and will abstain from killing. I will dwell meekly and kindly, compassionate and merciful to all beings, and lay aside both stick and sword. In this way I will follow the example of the saints and uphold the precepts.[22]

The fundamental rule of not taking life remains unchanged. But again the emphasis has shifted from the physical form of karmically significant acts and their consequences to the motives and attitudes that accompany action. The paradigm embodied in the ritual is now understood to be one of intentionality—being meek and kind, compassionate and merciful.

If purity and merit are not the principal rationales of nonviolence in the Buddhist system of values, then what is? The following passage from the *Mettā Sutta* suggests an answer:

May all beings be happy and secure in themselves, truly happy. All in whom breath of life exists—moving and unmoving, long, large, middle-sized, subtle and gross in form, visible and invisible, far and near, those who have been and those who will be—may all these be in themselves truly happy. Let none deceive another, nor despise another anywhere. Let none will ill to another because of dispute or enmity. In this way, as a mother protects her own child, her only child, as long as she lives, so should you develop an unlimited mind with respect to all beings. You should develop unlimited thoughts of sympathy for all beings in the world above, below, and across, unmarred by hate or enmity. Then, as you stand, walk, sit, or lie, love is ever present in the mind. This is called the holy state. When you hold on to opinions no more, when you are endowed with good conduct and true insight, when you have expelled all craving for pleasures, you will be reborn no more.[23]

This passage is more subtle than it may seem. If offers no motivation for compassion beyond compassion itself, nor any goal besides the happiness of living beings. Compassion is explicitly linked to the practice of meditation, on an equal level, and both are supposed to culminate in an "unlimited" mind with respect to all beings. Here the justification for nonviolence is peace and harmony among living beings, rather than purity or merit. Thus at least part of the rationale for nonviolence is to be found in the inherent worth of sentient beings and in the inherent value of a life with minimal suffering.

However, ideals such as "respect for life" or "fulfilling the aspirations of all living beings" do not provide an unambiguous guideline for behavior. These formulations overlook the diversity of life as well as the untamed conflict between living beings in their natural state. After all, the best way to make a tiger happy may be to feed it a lamb. Buddhist ethical thought, at least in its early stages, did not investigate this kind of problem. Since Buddhist lore tends to idealize all living beings by projecting onto them an anthropomorphic moral consciousness, they are perceived as having religious aspirations similar to those of human beings. Traditional Buddhist "animal stories" serve primarily as allegories for human conduct; often they are not even intended as statements about the feelings and needs of other forms of life.

As we saw in the hungry tigress story, Buddhism places a high moral value on self-sacrifice, even if the sacrifice is for a creature that we would normally conceive to be lower in the scale of being. And this, of course, raises further issues. I am not implying that because animals are lower in the scale of being they are therefore undeserving of our concern. The problem is that the acceptance of a certain responsibility for other forms of life does not answer the question of priorities or hierarchies. Why would the Bodhisattva, who was a very advanced being, sacrifice himself for a tigress? On the other hand, if one does establish a hierarchy, is the ranking of beings to be taken as a rule that overrides the principle of compassion? Some canonical passages advise Buddhists *not* to sacrifice themselves for an inferior living being. The usual example is a criminal rather than an animal.[24] If a criminal is trying to kill you, at that moment should you sacrifice yourself or not? What if the criminal's potential victim is a third person, and there is an opportunity for you to intervene? If a Buddhist claims that self-sacrifice is an inappropriate response to such a situation, then how does this accord with statements recommending that one sacrifice oneself for a tiger or another animal? What are the rules for establishing a hierarchy of living things? Buddhists (and Jains) proposed various theories: for example, the number of senses that a particular being possesses would determine its position in a scale used to measure the seriousness of an act of killing. Though such notions may offer a starting-point for inquiry, I do not think the Indian tradition adequately explored the implications of "respect for life" as a rationale for nonviolence.

Nonviolence and Self-cultivation

As we noted at the beginning of this chapter, the Buddhist ecology of mind encapsulates the world in the self. The centrality of self-cultivation is apparent throughout the texts of early Buddhism: in monastic codes, in *Jātaka* stories, in Aśoka's edicts, and in works that are ostensibly about ethics or ritual. Portraying a Buddhist monk, the *Mettā Sutta* says:

> He must be able and upright, truly upright, gentle in speech, kind and without conceit. He must be content, frugal, with few wants, free from care. His senses must be calm and discrete. He must be easily satisfied and never greedy when collecting alms. He would not do anything, however insignificant, that would meet with the censure of the wise.[25]

This is a classic description of a monk, quite similar to what one finds in the Western monastic tradition. The ideal is not abstract or mystical; rather, it centers on a ritualized mode of life, a morality of self-cultivation, that includes the way a monk walks, speaks, and so forth. This passage is followed, without any kind of transition, by the famous prayer "May all beings be happy," as quoted at length above. The proximity between the two suggests a close connection between the ordering of the mind and the welling up of compassion. It could be argued that one cannot have an ordered mind without the external practice of nonviolence; but I think the *Mettā Sutta* moves in the opposite direction: the compassionate practice of nonviolence requires an ordered mind. Nonviolence is part of a continuum from the mind to the world.

Beyond cultivating himself, the monk practices concern for others as well. In the Pali scriptures we find a number of passages that try to clarify the meaning of self-interest and concern for others. One text asks: "What kind of person torments the self? What kind of person torments others? What kind of person torments both self and others? And what kind of person torments neither self nor others?"[26] The person who torments only the self is, in the Indian context, a non-Buddhist ascetic, one who engages in extreme forms of self-mortification. Those who torment others include butchers, hunters, fishermen, bandits, executioners, jailers, and so on. Who are those who torment both self and others? Powerful men, such as kings: they torment others through their henchmen, and they torment themselves through lack of self-restraint. The person who does not cause injury or pain to anyone is, of course, the one who embodies the Buddhist ideal. This person is typically identified with the Buddhist monk and described in the following manner:

> He torments neither himself nor another, and his life is free of craving. He is calmed, he has become cool. . . . He has penetrated bliss, he lives with a self that has become Brahma. . . . He abandons the slaying of creatures, he abstains from killing. He lives as one who has laid down the rod, who has laid down the knife, who has scruples, who feels kindness and compassion for every living thing.[27]

Continuing its description of the person who will harm neither self nor other, the passage enumerates ten types of conduct for a monk to avoid. Killing is the first of these, followed by prohibitions against stealing, lying, and so on. Because all these actions produce pain, their prohibition is interpreted as a commandment of nonviolence. In this way the Buddhist moral code becomes a guideline for the expression of *ahiṃsā*. For the early Buddhists, it was as important to link these commandments with nonviolence as it was to link meditation with nonviolence.

Self and No-self

Buddhist self-cultivation is paradoxical, because one of its aims is the realization of no-self. Moreover, the tradition is able to contemplate nonviolence with equal facility in terms of self and in terms of no-self.

What is the connection between abstention, compassion, and nonviolence? What is the bridge between a morality that aims to keep one free from some kind of impurity and a morality that has the welfare of other living beings in mind? The key to this problem may be found in the general Buddhist doctrine of the self, and especially in the Buddhist understanding of the dialectic implicit in definitions of self and other.

One of the unique features of the Buddhist approach is the way in which nonviolence is related to the notion of no-self. Newcomers to Asian thought sometimes imagine that an emphasis on no-self removes all the motivations that anyone could have for really being concerned for others. Such a misinterpretation assumes that a person who has realized the ultimate illusoriness of the self can disregard the point of view of those who still believe in the self. But this is not the case. Even if one could become free from the idea of a self, one would certainly not assume that other people were free from their own habits of self. When someone "free of self" considers other people, he or she must still regard them from the point of view of the self.

Another misconception—that an experience of no-self somehow represents an escape from interpersonal reality—assumes that it is easy to be free from the idea of a self, perhaps through a simple inversion of cognitive patterns. Yet the self is the necessary reference point for the cultivation of no-self, as well as the focus for the cultivation of a nonviolent self. For instance, in *Suttanipāta* we read:

> The [true] ascetic thinks: "They [other living beings] are like myself, and I am like them." Thus, regarding them as like himself, he will not do violence to them, he will not cause harm to them.[28]

An ascetic who has retired to a mountain cave or a jungle hermitage still has the seeds of self within him. Understanding this "self," he knows the meaning of fear and pain, and he sees their effect on other living beings. He may be free from self in the sense that the pain of others becomes the center of his concern, and yet he still must use his own self as a reference point. A similar notion is expressed in a well-known stanza from the *Dhammapada*: "All beings fear violence, all fear death. Considering them like oneself, one will not do violence to others or cause them any harm."[29]

A complementary perspective on the question of self and other is developed in the *Saṃyutta Nikāya* in the form of a story. Pasenadi, the king of Kosala, strolls with his queen, Mallikā, to the upper terrace of his palace. Perhaps the King and the Queen had been having a pleasant evening walk, and now they stand looking down on their capital city, relaxing as the breeze begins to cool the heat of the day. In an intimate mood, King Pasenadi asks his wife: "Is there anyone who is more dear to you than yourself?" This is surely not meant as a philosophical inquiry; the King no doubt expects the Queen to reply, "You, of course, my dear." But the Queen is in a very frank mood, and she answers, "There is indeed no one more dear to me than myself." Then she returns the question to the King, asking, "Is there anyone who is more dear to you than yourself?" Her candor is disarming; the King has to be frank too. "I also know no one who is more dear to me than myself," he says.[30] Not long after this troubling conversation, the King sought the counsel of the Buddha:

> He approached the Blessed One, saluted him, and sat at his side. And when he was sitting at the Blessed One's side, Pasenadi, the king of Kosala, [recounted the conversation with his wife]. Then the Blessed One, understanding the true meaning of this, pronounced these inspired verses: "If you thoroughly search in ten directions with your mind, nowhere will you find anything more dear to you than yourself. In the same way, the self is extremely dear to others. Therefore, one who loves himself should cause no harm to another."[31]

These texts invite another shift in our perception of self and other. We have already seen one such shift, leading to an identification of self with others; now we have a second one, which is to understand that the basis for nonviolence, the basis for compassion, is love of self. It is not that the self has been reaffirmed or intensified, nor is it to be considered as an entity separate from its surroundings. What the passages indicate is that both reference points, self and other, are changed through the development of compassion and the practice of nonviolence. One source of this transformation is the elimination of one's own deeply ingrained preconceptions and habits. Another source is an empathetic awareness of the image others have of themselves.

The change in the perception of one's own self-image is further illustrated by the first of the four "Brahman Truths":

> A [true] Brahman says or thinks thus: "All living things are not to be harmed." So saying, a Brahman speaks truth, not falsehood. He has no conceit of recluse or brahmin, he has no conceit of better am I, equal am I, inferior am I. Moreover, by fully comprehending the truth contained in that saying, he is bent on the practice of mercy and compassion for all living beings.[32]

The passage makes two points. The obvious one is that the Brahman practices compassion; he does not harm living beings. Less obvious is the connection between this behavior and the idea that there is no conceit of "better am I, equal am I, inferior am I." The passage is suggesting, in other words, that compassion involves a change in self-perception or identity, in how the self is constituted and placed in the world. Normally, we experience the self as the center of the universe. The body, as the locus of perception, seems to perceive outward toward the world through our eyes and other sense organs, so we assume the center has to be somehow in this body. Not only do we perceive the self as the center of the world, we externalize other selves not as selves but as objects. Even when we experience self and others intersubjectively, we tend to rank other persons, living things, and objects in a hierarchy, generally placing our "own" self on the highest rung of the ladder.

The text of the Brahman Truths presents a different model of the relationship of self and others: neither low nor high. As a matter of fact, not even equal. The text implies that thinking, by comparing or ranking self and others, is at the root of suffering. As the story about King Pasenadi also suggested, to become aware of the self of others is most fulfilling and salutary when different selves are not compared.

Here we encounter the subtle interplay between self-definition and the self-cultivation that leads to no-self: I live the self of others in order not to have a self of my own. Ultimately, one cannot order one's life by the search for self-satisfaction. For one's own happiness often means the misery of another (at least from the standpoint of conventional truth). One can create a new order for the self only by understanding that both self and other derive their value from the same source. The shorthand expression "no-self" refers to a state of consciousness in which the advancement of the self is subordinated to the principle of not harming others, and self-identity is actualized in accepting others as a self.

Our examination of the Pali scriptures and related sources has demonstrated that there was not just one unalloyed ideal of nonviolence in early Buddhism. Instead we encountered several definitions and redefinitions of *ahiṃsā*. As ritual thinking was rationalized and ethicized, a tradition of nonviolence as abstention vied with a tradition of nonviolence based on a valuation of life. In many cases, abstention was regarded as ethically equivalent to involvement, and the practice of nonviolence was motivated as much by an ideal of self-realization as by an ideal of cosmic healing.

We also found that the close connection between self-cultivation and nonviolence, an essential feature of early Buddhism, raises important questions about the role of the self. As a ritual symbol, nonviolence serves as a mechanism for constructing or maintaining a self-image. In other contexts as well, nonviolence involves self-assertion as much as self-denial. It might be said that the self that is asserted is that of all beings. Yet the individual self, first split into self and other, then reintegrated in the experience of no-self, is what gives meaning to the concept of all beings, and to the activity of nonviolence.

While not harming and no-self are the fundamental guidelines of Buddhist ethics, the specific application of these guidelines is not always clear. How are we to deal with the problems that arise when we try to implement the principles of nonviolence in our daily lives or in larger social contexts? What about situations in which avoiding violence may lead to the suffering of others? How about cases where justice seems to require vio-

lence? Buddhist texts address some of these issues but leave others unre-
solved. In the *Avataṃsaka Sūtra* (which unfortunately has no early counterpart), a paradox is used to define the Buddhist ideal of altruism: "The
bodhisattva will not give up one single living being for the sake of all beings, nor will he give up all beings for the sake of one living being."[33]
What distinguishes (or should distinguish) advocates of nonviolence
who identify themselves with Buddhist teachings is a recognition of the indispensable link between nonviolence and self-cultivation. The Vinaya
rules imply that nonviolence forms part of a morality of abstention, in
which one's own daily behavior is the starting-point of any campaign for
peace. Refraining from lying, for example, would take precedence over
public verbal activities such as issuing proclamations in support of world
harmony (or writing essays on *ahiṃsā*). Similarly, it may be more valuable
to recycle one's recyclable trash on a regular basis than to join marches on
behalf of the environment. Even working in a crisis center for victims of
family violence might still represent a step outside the primary arena of
concern. The core of Buddhist nonviolence is a very humble kind of practice. Its basis is not harming, not stealing, not lying, and so on.

If ethical behavior could be governed by principles that would provide, in all circumstances, an unambiguously moral and rational course of
action, then self-cultivation would center on compliance, and we would no
longer be able to speak of virtue. But Buddhist self-cultivation nurtures a
kind of virtue that transcends mere compliance with moral principles.
Thus when Buddhists speaks of a buddha or a saint, they say that he or she
has gone beyond merit and demerit, beyond good and evil, beyond self
and other, "beyond the heavens and the hells." For those who have at-
tained this state, "love is ever present in the mind."[34]

Notes

Several of the translations quoted in this chapter have been modified
slightly to conform to contemporary usage. In the following notes, PTS =
Pali Text Society Publications.

1. Compare Gregory Bateson, *Steps to an Ecology of Mind* (New York: Bal-
   lantine, 1972), 460ff. A Buddhist ecology of mind encompasses even
   more than Bateson's "integrated network."
2. Hendrik Kern, ed., *Ārya Śūra: Jātakamālā*, Harvard Oriental Series,
   vol. 1 (Cambridge: Harvard University Press, 1890), 181ff. See also J.
   A. Speyer, trans., *Ārya Śūra's Jātakamālā*, Sacred Books of the Buddhists, vol. 1 (London: Henry Frowde, 1895).
3. Kern, *Ārya Śūra: Jātakamālā*, 1ff.
4. N. A. Nikam and Richard McKeon, trans., *The Edicts of Aśoka* (Chicago:

University of Chicago Press, 1959), 55. See also Jules Bloch, ed., *Les In-scriptions d'Aśoka* (Paris: Les Belles Lettres, 1950), 92–93.

5. Bloch, *Les Inscriptions d'Aśoka*, 97. Here, as in most places in the Edicts, the word for not destroying life is *anārambha* (or one of its cognates). Aśoka did not know the word *ahiṃsā*, although he sometimes used the synonym *avihiṃsā*.

6. Ibid., 166.

7. Ibid., 166.

8. Ibid., 94.

9. For a summary of research on the texts known to Aśoka, see Etienne Lamotte, *Histoire du bouddhisme indien* (Louvain: Institut Orientaliste, 1958), 256ff.

10. Nikam and McKeon, *The Edicts of Aśoka*, 40 (modified slightly).

11. See, for instance, *Aṅguttara Nikāya*, PTS 1:205–211.

12. W. Norman Brown, "The Sanctity of the Cow in Hinduism," *Journal of the Madras University* 28 (1957), 29–49. See also D. Seyfort Ruegg, "*Ahiṃsā* and Vegetarianism in the History of Buddhism," in S. Balasooriya, et al., *Buddhist Studies in Honor of Walpola Rahula* (London: Gordon Fraser, 1980), 234–41.

13. This is a non-Pali version. Takakusu Junjirō, et al., *Taishō shinshū daizōkyō* (Tokyo: Daizō Shuppan, 1924–32), no. 1509, 159b–c. Cf. *Aṅguttara Nikāya*, PTS 1:211–12.

14. See, for example, *Bṛhadāranyaka Upaniṣad* I.5.14.

15. Nikam and McKeon, *The Edicts of Aśoka*, 56.

16. Takakusu, *Taishō shinshū daizōkyō*, no. 1509, 159b–c.

17. *Aṅguttara Nikāya*, PTS 2:72–73.

18. Ibid., 73.

19. Padmanabh S. Jaini, *The Jaina Path of Purification* (Berkeley: University of California Press, 1979), 112.

20. "Absorbed" is my rendering of the term *āsrava*, which originally meant "to flow in." Theravada commentators (and early Western translators) misconstrued the term as "outflow."

21. *Dhammapada*, PTS, 141–42. See also the rejection of purity (*visuddhi*) as a goal in *Aṅguttara Nikāya*, PTS 5:64.

22. *Aṅguttara Nikāya*, PTS 1:211.

23. *Mettā Sutta*, in *Suttanipāta*, PTS I:8, 143–52.

24. Paul Demiéville, "*Le bouddhisme et la guerre*," in *Choix d'études boud-dhiques (1929–1970)* (Leiden: E. J. Brill, 1973), 261–99.

25. *Mettā Sutta*, in *Suttanipāta*, PTS I:8, 143–52.

26. *Aṅguttara Nikāya*, PTS 2:205–211.

27. Ibid., 208–209.

28. *Suttanipāta* PTS III.11, 704–705.

29. *Saṃyutta Nikāya*, PTS, 129–30.
30. *Saṃyutta Nikāya*, PTS 1:75.
31. Ibid., 75.
32. *Aṅguttara Nikāya*, PTS 2:176.
33. Takakusu, *Taishō shinshū daizōkyō*, no. 279, 106c.
34. *Mettā Sutta*, in *Suttanipāta*, PTS I:8, 143–52.

3

Nonviolence to Animals in Buddhism and Jainism

by Christopher Chapple

By extending the principle of nonviolence to the animal realm, Buddhism offers a distinctive perspective on the role of animals in the drama of human life. The view of animals that developed in traditional Indian culture differs radically from the attitudes toward animals that are commonly held in the West. Noninjury to living beings is a cardinal precept in Buddhism and Jainism, and this single tenet exerted considerable influence throughout Central Asia, China, Korea, Japan, and Southeast Asia. The Indian worldview also embraces the notion of repeated, cyclical embodiment, as described by the Sanskrit word *saṃsāra*: "passing through a succession of states." While interpretations of nonviolence vary, we will focus here on the related concepts of noninjury and rebirth as they apply to animals in the Jain and Buddhist traditions. At the close of the discussion we will consider how these religions might address a contemporary issue related to animals—their use in scientific research.

Nonviolence in Jainism

Jainism is one of the most ancient traditions of India. The name Jainism is derived from the term *jina*, which means conqueror or victor. The Jains are followers of the path established by the Jinas, those who have conquered the suffering (*duḥkha*) inherent in attachment. The most recent

49

Jina, Vardhamāna Mahāvīra, is said to have lived from 599 B.C.E. to 527 B.C.E. His predecessor Pārśvanatha has been dated to 850 B.C.E. At the heart of Jainism is the doctrine that all being is divided into nonliving (*ajīva*) and living (*jīva*) forms. The former includes what we might consider principles: motion, rest, space, matter, and time. Living forms include almost everything regarded as animate or inanimate by non-Jains, from a rock and a drop of water to men and women. Each life form, including mountains, lakes, and trees, is said to have consciousness, bliss, and energy. Living beings are classified in a hierarchical fashion according to the number of senses they possess. Earth, water, fire, air, and vegetables, the simplest forms of life, are said to possess only the sense of touch. Worms have both touch and taste. Bugs, lice, and ants have touch, taste, and smell; moths, bees, and flies add the sense of seeing. Snakes possess all the senses, including hearing, while beasts, birds, fish, and humans are said to have six senses: seeing, hearing, tasting, smelling, touching, and thinking.[1] Hence the human order is, technically speaking, equivalent to that of fish and animals.

A living form's status in this hierarchy is not fixed but is in a constant state of flux, indicated by the term *saṃsāra*. The universe is filled with living beings that have no beginning; driven by unquenched desires, they continually take on new embodiments. These embodiments or states of being fall into four categories: gods, humans, hell beings, and animals and plants. The last of these—animals and plants—is divided into three parts, the lowest form of life being the *nigoda*, which "are so undifferentiated that they lack even individual bodies; large clusters of them are born together as colonies that die a fraction of a second later."[2] They are said to reside in flesh, among other places. Above these are the earth bodies, the water bodies, the fire bodies, and the air bodies. The third and highest division of this plant and animal group includes plants and the various beasts just mentioned.

The most important state to achieve is that of a human being, as it is the only state in which living forms (*jīva*) can be freed from the bondage of action (karma). For the Jains, karma is a physical entity, a viscous mass that adheres to the *jīva* and causes attachment and suffering. The average person is filled with karma, which obstructs one's true nature of infinite knowledge, bliss, and energy. The influx of new karma must cease if a person is to achieve the pinnacle of all life, a state of liberation beyond attachment to passion and impurity.

In order to overcome the negative influence of karma, Jains embrace a series of vows. The first and foremost of these is the vow of noninjury (*ahiṃsā*). The word *ahiṃsā* comes from the Sanskrit root *hiṃs*, a desiderative form of the verb *han*, to kill or injure or strike. Prefixed with the privative "*a*," it can be translated as "absence of the desire to kill or harm."[3] This is the prime practice in Jainism for overcoming past actions, so all dimensions of the religion reflect a concern for *ahiṃsā*. Acts of violence are to be avoided because they will result in injury to oneself at some future time, perhaps even in another embodiment. The *Ācārāṅga Sūtra* states the need for *ahiṃsā* as follows:

> Injurious activities inspired by self-interest lead to evil and darkness. This is what is called bondage, delusion, death, and hell. To do harm to others is to do harm to oneself. "You are the person whom you want to kill! You are the person whom you want to tyrannize!" We corrupt ourselves as soon as we intend to corrupt others. We kill ourselves as soon as we intend to kill others.[4]

In order to uphold the vows of *ahiṃsā*, two paths of practice were developed: one for Jain monks, who adhere to greater vows, and another for Jain laypeople, who follow a less rigorous discipline. Four types of violence were acknowledged: intentional, nonintentional, related to profession, and self-defense. The monks live according to rules that avoid all types of violence; laypersons are allowed to take life in some instances. All Jains are strict vegetarians, living solely on one-sensed beings (vegetables) and milk products. Alcohol, honey, and certain kinds of figs are also prohibited, because they are said to harbor many forms of life, especially the undeveloped *nigoda*.

Ahiṃsā is practiced in five ways: restraint of mind, control of tongue, carefulness on roads, removing beings from the road, and eating in daylight (to avoid ingesting bugs). In order to observe these forms of *ahiṃsā*, several rules are required, including care in movement, speech, eating, placing and removing, and evacuation. An additional rule limits the area of one's activities, in an attempt to reduce the potential harm one may cause in far-off places. Strong prohibitions against travel by monks have contributed to the regional nature of Jainism. These concerns have led the Jain community to pursue limited means of livelihood: government and farming are acceptable but not desirable occupations; writing, arts, and crafts are encouraged; and commerce is the most desirable, as long as the trade is not conducted in tools of violence. For the most advanced monks the disciplines become increasingly rigorous: limited food intake, restraint from sexual desire, and the renunciation of all possessions (in one sect, any form of clothing is renounced). No digging, bathing, lighting or extinguishing of fires, or fanning is allowed in order to protect earth, water, fire, and air bodies, respectively.

Jains have long protested against the Hindu practice of animal sacrifice. One text declares: "Those terrible ones who kill animals under the guise of making an offering to the gods, or the guise of sacrifice, are bereft of compassion and go to a bad fate."[5] The Jain monk Hīravijaya-Sūri persuaded the Muslim emperor Akbar (1556–1605) to prohibit the killing of animals on certain days. Akbar eventually renounced hunting and changed his own eating habits. Largely as a result of Jain efforts, vegetarianism can be found in all parts of India, and animal sacrifice is now illegal in most regions.

These prohibitions are primarily statements about what *not* to do, and they convey little of the affection most Jains hold for animals. There are numerous Jain stories in which animals make choices or act compassionately, behavior that subsequently advances them from animal to human status. One such story concerns a kindhearted elephant:

> Long ago, there was a large forest fire, and all the animals of the forest fled and gathered around a lake, including deer, rabbits, squirrels, and a herd of elephants. For hours the animals crowded together in their small refuge, cowering from the fire. The leader of the elephant herd got an itch and he raised a leg to scratch himself. A tiny rabbit quickly occupied the space vacated by the elephant's foot. The elephant, out of an unwavering desire not to hurt the rabbit, stood on three legs for more than three days until the fire died down and the rabbit scampered off. By then, his leg was numb and he toppled over. Still retaining a pure mind and heart, the elephant died. As a reward for his compassion he overcame the need for embodiment as an animal and was born as a prince by the name of Megha, who eventually became a disciple of Mahāvīra. Taking the vows of monkhood, he aspired to transcend all forms of existence.[6]

Clearly, the worldview of the Jains is grounded in an unparalleled concern for life. "All beings are fond of life, like pleasure, hate pain, shun destruction, like life, long to live. To all life is dear."[7] Though Jains have remained a tiny minority in India, they have exerted considerable influence on Indian society over the centuries.

Treatment of Animals in Buddhism

Like Jainism, Buddhism originated in India as a religious movement distinguishable from Hinduism in its nonallegiance to Vedic texts and in its disdain for animal sacrifice. Although Buddhism does not posit a permanent self-nature, it does accept karma as the force that causes the continuation of *saṃsāra*. In Buddhism, *saṃsāra* is divided into six domains. Depending on one's past and present actions, one may be born as an animal, a hungry ghost, a denizen of hell, a fighting titan, a human being, or a god. Birth as an animal, regarded as punishment for evil deeds, plunges one into a realm of fear, misery, and slaughter. A representative text states:

> As a rule, through cupidity one becomes a spirit [hungry ghost]; through malevolence one is born in hell; through deludedness one becomes an animal.... By constantly committing evil deeds we are reborn in hell, by doing many we become spirits, and when we do only a few we are reborn as an animal.[8]

Graphic stories have been told to communicate the need to act properly to avoid birth as an animal. In the *Avadāna Śataka*, a group of lazy and indolent students are reborn as parrots and swans "as a punishment for their indifference to duty." Another student who fails to keep a fast is reborn as a snake.[9] Though animalhood is a possible alternative to human existence, in these contexts animal existence is not regarded as a desirable state by Buddhists.

At the same time, animals are also presented in a positive manner in Buddhist literature. For instance, in the *Jātakamālā*, didactic tales told by the Buddha, he portrays himself in his former lives as a rabbit, a swan, a fish, a quail, an ape, a woodpecker, an elephant, and a deer. The sufferings of both beast and man help initiate his quest for awakening. In one such story, the future Buddha nurses back to health a goose that had been shot by his cousin Devadatta. In another tale, he feels compassion when he sees a tired farmer plowing the earth, a bird eating a worm dredged up by the plow, the welts inflicted on the back of the ox by the farmer, and the weariness of both the gaunt farmer and the overworked ox.

In some instances in Buddhist literature, animals are portrayed as sacrificing their lives for the sake of human beings. In other cases, humans give up their own flesh and sometimes their very lives so that animals may survive. The *Avadāna-kalpalatā* tells of an elephant who throws himself off a rock in the desert to rescue starving travelers. A lion and an elephant rescue some men from a dragon, sacrificing their lives in the process.[10] In the *Śaśa Jātaka*, a rabbit offers his body to a Brahman for food, jumping into a fire that the rabbit had piled up himself. (The Brahman was the god Indra in disguise; later he placed a figure of the rabbit in the moon.)[11] But these stories are only half of the picture. Several parables and birth stories tell of humans sacrificing their flesh so that animals may keep living. Other contributors to this volume discuss the well-known story in which the future Buddha throws himself before a hungry tigress so that she may feed her cubs. The sixteenth minor precept in the *Fan-wang-ching* (*Brahmajāla Sūtra*), a text popular in China, graphically states that "One should be willing to forsake one's entire body, one's flesh, hands, and feet as an offering to starving tigers, wolves, lions, and hungry ghosts."[12] However overstated this passage may sound, the message is clear that animals are to be treated with great respect.

The treatment of animals is included in the first Buddhist precept—not to harm or injure living things. In some instances, the qualifier "intentionally" is added to this precept. In the *Mahāvagga*, the Buddha proclaims: "A *bhikkhu* [monk] who has received ordination ought not intentionally to destroy the life of any living being down to a worm or an ant."[13] This concern for animals was sometimes extended to plants as well. In the early days of the Buddhist community, the monks traveled throughout the year. The public, however, protested that "they crush the green herbs, they hurt vegetable life, they destroy the life of many small living beings," particularly when traveling during the rainy season.[14] Subsequently, the Buddha required that all the monks enter retreats and stop wandering during the monsoons.

The Mahayana tradition elaborates on the first precept in various ways. The *Daśabhūmika Sūtra* states that a Buddhist "must not hate any being and cannot kill a living creature even in thought."[15] In an eleventh-century text Kṣemendra writes, "I cannot endure the pain even of an ant."[16] In the *Bodhisattva-bhūmi* discussion of giving (*dāna*), the first of the six perfections (*pāramitā*), the Buddhist is not allowed to give anything that "may be used to inflict injury on other living beings," nor is he allowed to give "poisons, weapons, intoxicating liquors, and nets for the capture of animals. He should not bestow on others a piece of land on which the animals may be hunted or killed."[17]

One *Jātaka* tale is particularly instructive in regard to the importance of noninjury to life:

Once upon a time, a goat was led to a temple and was about to be sacrificed by the presiding Brahman. Suddenly the goat let out a laugh and then uttered a moaning cry. The Brahman, startled by this odd behavior, asked the goat what was happening. The goat responded as follows: "Sir, I have just remembered the history of what has led to this event. The reason I have laughed is that I realized that this is the last of five hundred births I have suffered as a goat; in my next life I will return again as a human. The reason I have cried is out of compassion for you. You see, five hundred births ago I was a Brahman, leading a goat to the sacrifice. After killing the goat, I was condemned to five hundred births as a goat. If you kill me, you will suffer the same fate." The Brahman, visibly shaken, immediately released the goat, who trotted away. A few minutes later, lightning struck the goat and he was freed to become human again. The Brahman likewise was spared, due to the goat's compassionate intervention.[18]

This story alludes to several Buddhist teachings, including karma, rebirth, noninjury, and compassion. Perhaps its graphic indictment of animal sacrifice also served a polemic function in Buddhism's attempt to distance itself from Hinduism.

Animal Protection in Buddhism

The concern for animal welfare was not confined to the Buddhist monastic community. The Indian king Aśoka (third century B.C.E.) converted to Buddhism and established several laws that required kind treatment of animals. These included restricting meat consumption, curtailing hunting, and establishing hospitals and roadside watering stations for animals. Many of Aśoka's inscriptions have been preserved on rocks and pillars still standing throughout India. Numerous passages deal with animals:

> Hundred of thousands of living creatures were formerly slaughtered every day for curries in the kitchens of his Majesty, Beloved of the Gods, of Sweet Countenance. As this edict is being inscribed, only three living beings are killed daily: two peacocks and one deer. And the deer is not slaughtered regularly. In the future, not even these three animals will be slaughtered. (Rock Edict I)

> Everywhere [the King] has established provisions for two kinds of medical treatment: treatment of men, and treatment of animals. Wherever the proper medicinal herbs suitable for men and animals were lacking, they have been imported and planted. Also, where roots and fruits were lacking, they have been imported and planted. . . . Wells have been dug, and trees have been planted, for the use of animals and men. (Rock Edict II)

> On bipeds and quadrupeds, on birds and aquatic animals, various benefits have been conferred by me [even] as far as the grant of life. (Pillar Edict II)

> The Beloved of the Gods spoke thus:

> Twenty-six years after my coronation, I declare that the following animals are not to be killed: parrots, mynas, the *aruṇa*, ruddy geese, wild ducks, the *nandīmukha*, the *gelāta*, bats, queen ants, small tortoises, boneless fish, the *vedaveyaka*, the *Gaṅgā-pupuṭaka*, the *sankuja* fish, large tortoises and porcupines, squirrels, young deer, bulls, the *okapiṇḍa*, wild asses, white pigeons, village pigeons, and all quadrupeds which are neither useful nor edible.

> Those she-goats and sows that are pregnant or are in milk, also the young less than six months, are inviolable.

Cocks are not to be caponised.

Husks containing living beings [i.e., insects] are not to be burnt.

Forests are not to be burnt, either uselessly or for killing animals.

One animal is not to be fed with another animal.

Fish must not be killed or sold on the day of the full moon which begins each of the three seasons, on the Tiṣya [Sirius] full moon, on the three days which end a fortnight and begin a new one, or on fast days [a total of fifty-six days during each year].

And on those same days one is not to kill other animals that live in the elephant forest and the fisheries.

On [designated days] and on auspicious days, bulls, he-goats, rams, boars, and other animals that are usually castrated must not be castrated.

On [designated days], the branding of horses and bullocks is not to be done. (Pillar Edict V)[19]

Though in many ways only a partial assertion of animals rights, these inscriptions nonetheless reveal an unusual degree of compassion on the part of a temporal ruler toward his subjects, both human and animal.

This policy of animal protection spread with Buddhism to China and Japan, where it periodically gained favor as a means of earning merit. The twentieth precept of the *Fan-wang-ching* (*Brahmajāla Sūtra*) declares:

If one is a son of Buddha, one must, with a merciful heart, intentionally practice the work of liberating living beings. All men are our fathers, all women are our mothers. All our existences have taken birth from them.

Therefore all living beings of the six realms are our parents, and if we kill them, we kill our parents and also our former bodies.

Therefore one must always practice liberation of living beings and cause others to do so; if one sees a worldly person kill animals, one must by proper means save and protect these animals and free them from their misery and danger.[20]

The influence of this and other texts such as the *Suvarnaprabhāṣa Sūtra* caused Chinese and Japanese leaders to promote the institution of "meetings for liberating living beings" (Chinese: *fang-shêng-hui*; Japanese: *hōjō-e*). In the sixth century the monk Chi-i reportedly convinced more than a thousand fishermen to give up their work. He also purchased an extensive tract of land as a protected area where animals could be released. In the mid-eighth century a Chinese emperor established eighty-one ponds where fish could be released, and subsequent emperors embraced similar measures. In Japan, Emperor Temmu restricted the use of certain hunting devices and the eating of cow, horse, dog, and monkey meat (675 C.E.), and he ordered that various provinces "let loose living things" the following year. In 741 Emperor Shōmu ordered prohibitions against hunting and fishing on the fast days of the month. His daughter, Empress Kōken, issued several similar decrees.[21] The release of living beings continues to be practiced in the East Asian world, primarily as a ceremonial event.[22]

Although vegetarianism is not a strict requirement for all Buddhist monastic communities, some sects emphasize the importance of not eating meat. The *Lankāvatāra Sūtra*, one of the early texts of the Mahayana school (and especially linked to Zen Buddhism), makes an earnest appeal for vegetarianism and respect for animals in its eighth chapter. It states in part:

> In the long course of *saṃsāra*, there is not one among living beings with form who has not been mother, father, brother, sister, son or daughter, or some other relative. Being connected with the process of taking birth, one is kin to all wild and domestic animals, birds, and beings born from the womb.[23]

The view that all life is interrelated was used in this way to promote abstention from meat and to condemn maltreatment of animals.

In the present era, many Buddhists continue to take animals into consideration when stressing the sanctity of all life. The Dalai Lama articulates the Buddhist view with his usual clarity:

> In our approach to life, be it pragmatic or otherwise, a basic fact that confronts us squarely and unmistakably is the desire for peace, security, and happiness. Different forms of life at different levels of existence make up the teeming denizens of this earth of ours. And, no matter whether they belong to the higher groups such as human beings or to the lower groups such as animals, all beings primarily need peace, comfort, and security. Life is as dear to a mute creature as it is to man. Even the lowliest insect strives for protection against dangers that threaten its life. Just as each one of us wants happiness and fears pain, just as each one of us wants to live and not to die, so do all other creatures.[24]

A Contemporary Issue: Animals in Scientific Research

Though animal sacrifice in the name of religion is no longer a widespread practice, contemporary cultures commonly sacrifice animals in the name of scientific and medical progress. How might the classical Jain and Buddhist traditions respond to the current debate over the use and abuse of animals for scientific research? Of course, scientific research using animals did not exist when these traditions generated their seminal texts; nor is it a simple matter to extrapolate principles from one cultural milieu and apply them to a very different context.

Early Hindu communities performed intricate rituals that culminated in the sacrifice of live animals. For example, they released a horse for one year, followed it as it wandered throughout the land, then killed and dismembered it. For years, Buddhists and Jains labored against all types of animal sacrifice, using the argument that such activities violated the first and most important ethical principle: nonviolence. As we have seen, both traditions view animals as sentient beings. According to some of the parables cited above, animals also have feelings and emotions and are able to improve themselves. In this view, the entire human and animal kingdom becomes an extended family. For the Jains, even rocks and streams are within the same continuum. To kill therefore results in future suffering for oneself and others.

The doctrine of karma does not dwell upon the effects of human action on society, though threats of karmic punishment are used to advocate socially acceptable behavior. A modern reading of karma (which might not require belief in reincarnation) would be to view it as horizontal instead of sequential. An action does not necessarily remain confined to one life, because its influence spreads out to the lives of others. Actions by scientists affect society at large, often in unforeseen ways. The rise of science has given birth to medicines and comforts that have greatly eased human misery. But accompanying these same advances are threats of nuclear and chemical warfare, increased rates of cancer and heart disease, and tragedies such as thalidomide and agent orange. The violence that was required for the development of these various technologies and substances is now being experienced both directly and indirectly. Thus a Buddhist or Jain critique of scientific experimentation on animals might begin with an assessment of its karmic implications—for the animals, for the scientists, and for society.

Despite the abnegation of animal sacrifice by the Buddhists and the Jains, both traditions affirm the nobleness of animals and humans who give their lives to others, as seen in the story of the elephant who spared the rabbit or the story of the rabbit who jumped into the fire to feed a traveler. It might be construed that these anecdotes legitimize the loss of animal life for the sake of science. But in each of the stories the animals were not coerced into their acts of compassion; rather, they surrendered their lives out of their own will and desire. If such stories were recreated in a modern context, they would depict animals volunteering to overdose on drugs or be injected with carcinogens.

It might be argued that medicines are needed to protect the human order, that we are waging a war against disease and we need to enlist the aid of animals in a just war. The Jains, as we have seen, do include within their system a provision for committing violence out of self-defense. A Jain monk would try not to place himself in a situation that would require such an activity, but laypersons continually encounter a need for violence, however subtle, in order to survive. Would the threat of a disease that could only be counteracted by medicines tested on animals be an acceptable justification for restricted violence in "self-defense"? The Jain philosophy of nonabsolutism, an outgrowth of the *ahiṃsā* doctrine, would not allow a Jain to hold a rigid attitude about this or any other situation. A Jain would probably not deny that the scientist who conducts such experiments has a legitimate viewpoint within a scientific milieu.

However, the Jain precepts would prohibit a Jain from accepting the utility of killing animals for himself or herself. Because of the doctrines of karma and *ahiṃsā*, the Jain would refuse to be directly involved. He or she may follow the example of earlier Jains and attempt to make the other side see the validity of the Jain perspective and perhaps, at a minimum, declare days of abstinence from destruction. In fact, the Jain community, which controls the pharmaceutical industry in India, has put into practice a compromise solution to the problem of violence to laboratory animals. The animals are used for testing, but are then "rehabilitated" through shelters and recuperation facilities maintained by the laboratories. Whenever possible, those who recover are released back into the wild.[25]

From a Buddhist perspective, the endeavors of experimental science might be regarded as useful in a limited way, being primarily concerned with manipulations on the level of *saṃsāra*. From an ultimate point of view, such work would be more difficult to justify. Neither scientists nor disease victims nor animals have independent self-natures. All are composed of parts and are subject to decay and dissolution. All three need to be helped, not merely to live longer or more comfortably, but also to see their nonsubstantiality, their impermanence. For the Buddhist, avoidance of death, the *telos* of the scientific realm, would not be the highest value. Rather, the quality of death is most important, and it depends largely upon one's understanding of life. This is not to say that Buddhism looks forward to death; we have already noted many passages that affirm the sanctity of life. Aśoka instituted the planting of medicinal herbs for both animals and humans. Medical and surgical cures are mentioned in the early Buddhist canon, and later Buddhism includes healing deities who assist in curative processes.[26] But when death becomes imminent it must be accepted, and a Buddhist attempts to die freely, without attachment or fear.

How, then, might the Buddhist religion approach the modern practice of killing animals in research laboratories? Before passing judgment on any issue, Buddhism traditionally requires that three factors be taken into consideration: the intention of the act, the means used to execute it, and its consequences. Similar considerations could be used by a contemporary Buddhist to assess the killing of animals in research laboratories. The first category, intention, eliminates many possible circumstances, from destruction of animals for instruction in high school biology classes to research conducted by cosmetic companies catering to human vanity. Only in an extreme case would the intention be deemed acceptable, such as testing of a vaccine desperately needed to stave off an epidemic. Then the means would have to be considered. Can pain be minimized? Are the animals well-treated? Finally, the likely consequences must be weighed. Will lives in fact be saved? Will other reactions occur, such as genetic damage or increased risk of cancer? Will the test merely lead to the proliferation of more tests, thereby endangering more lives?

Buddhist leaders and organizations in North America continue to explore the issue of animal welfare. Roshi Philip Kapleau, founder of the Rochester Zen Center in upstate New York, has written the thoughtful book *To Cherish All Life: A Buddhist Case for Becoming Vegetarian*. A California-based organization called Buddhists Concerned for Animals (BCA) lobbies for animal rights in farming, scientific experimentation, war research, and trapping. Though such movements are operating on a small scale, they have the potential to influence larger numbers. The BCA's charter asserts:

> As Buddhist monks and laypeople, we are finding ourselves able to reach people who may otherwise not be involved in the effort to liberate animals from suffering. We aim to point out the relationship of the current animal rights movement to the traditional Buddhist path, and to a sometimes overlooked but present aspect in other religions.[27]

In India, the gentle persuasion of the Buddhists and Jains has convinced major segments of the population that the protection of living beings is meritorious and desirable. Similar efforts in the modern world may prove equally effective.[28]

Notes

1. Section 43, *Puruṣārtha-siddyupāya* of Amritchandra, trans. Ajit Prasada (Lucknow: Abhinadan, 1933).
2. *Gommaṭasāra-Jīvakāṇḍa*, in Padmanabh S. Jaini, *The Jaina Path of Purification* (Berkeley: University of California Press, 1979), 109.
3. Louis Dummont, *Homo Hierarchicus: The Caste System and Its Implications* (Chicago: University of Chicago Press, 1970), 148.

4. *Ācārāṅga Sūtra* I.1.2, I.5.5, in Nathmal Tatia, *Studies in Jaina Philosophy* (Banaras: Jain Cultural Research Society, 1951), 18 (modified).

5. Hemacandra, *Yogaśāstra*, II.39 (Mumbai, India: Jainasahityavik-asamandala, 1977).

6. This traditional story was told to me by Professor Padmanabh Jaini.

7. *Ācārāṅga Sūtra* I.2.3, in *Jaina Sūtras*, trans. Hermann Jacobi (New York: Dover Publications, 1968), 19.

8. Sgam-po-pa, *The Jewel Ornament of Liberation*, trans. Herbert Guenther (Berkeley: Shambhala, 1971), 79.

9. Har Dayal, *The Bodhisattva Doctrine in Buddhist Sanskrit Literature* (London: Kegan, Paul, Trench, Trubner, and Co., 1931), 221.

10. Dayal, *The Bodhisattva Doctrine*, 187.

11. "Animals," in *Encyclopedia of Buddhism*, ed. G. P. Malalasekara (Ceylon: Government Press, 1965), fascicle 4, 667–72.

12. *The Buddha Speaks the Brahma Net Sūtra*, trans. Dharma Realm Buddhist University (Talmage, Calif.: Buddhist Text Translation Society, 1981), 150.

13. *Mahāvagga* I.78.4, in *Vinaya Texts*, trans. T. W. Rhys-Davids and Hermann Oldenberg (Delhi: Motilal Banarasidass, 1974).

14. *Mahāvagga* III.1.1, in *Vinaya Texts*.

15. Dayal, *The Bodhisattva Doctrine*, 199.

16. Ibid, 199.

17. Ibid, 175.

18. *Jātaka* tale 18, retold from *Jātaka Tales*, H. T. Francis and E. J. Thomas, eds. (Cambridge: Cambridge University Press, 1916), 20–22.

19. For translations of Aśoka's edicts, see Amulyachandra Sen, *Aśoka's Edicts* (Calcutta: The Institute of Indology, 1956); N. A. Nikam and Richard McKeon, trans., *The Edicts of Aśoka* (Chicago: University of Chicago Press, 1959); and Jules Bloch, *Les Inscriptions d'Aśoka* (Paris: Les Belles Lettres, 1950).

20. M. W. deVisser, *Ancient Buddhism in Japan: Sūtras and Ceremonies in Use in the Seventh and Eighth Centuries A.D. and Their History in Later Times* (Leiden: E. J. Brill, 1935), 198.

21. deVisser, *Ancient Buddhism in Japan*, 198–212.

22. Holmes Welch, *The Practice of Chinese Buddhism, 1900–1950* (Cambridge: Harvard University Press, 1967), 378–82.

23. *Laṅkāvatāra Sūtra*, chapter 8, section 245.

24. Tenzin Gyatso, the 14th Dalai Lama, *Universal Responsiblity and the Good Heart* (Dharamsala, India: Library of Tibetan Works and Archives, 1980), 78.

25. *Ahiṃsā:* Nonviolence," Michael Tobias, executive producer, Public Broadcasting Service, 1986.

26. For a discussion of Buddhist medical practices, see Raoul Birnbaum, *The Healing Buddha* (Boulder: Shạmbhala, 1979).

27. "The Practice of Non-Injury," Buddhists Concerned for Animals, San Francisco, 1984.

28. An earlier version of this essay appeared in Tom Regan, ed., *Animal Sacrifices: Religious Perspectives on the Use of Animals in Science* (Philadelphia: Temple Unversity Press, 1986). Reprinted by permission of Temple University Press.

4

Exemplars of Nonviolence in Theravada Buddhism

by Donald K. Swearer

How can peace be promoted through nonviolent social change? In today's world this question has become so critical that we must use all available resources to grapple with it. I believe the Buddhist tradition can contribute to this common task in unique and important ways. Its principles, symbols, and moral exemplars have a proven capacity to inform and transform people, regardless of cultural or religious background. Buddhists in the late twentieth century have a responsibility to (re)discover how their tradition can help individuals realize peace, not only in their own lives but also in the world community.

It would be unwise, however, to assume that Buddhist followers have some kind of privileged status in regard to nonviolence. While Buddhists may not have tarnished world history by launching armed crusades to convert "pagan hordes," the historical record certainly shows that Buddhists—monks and laymen alike—have at times condoned, promoted, and participated in violence. To regard Buddhism as more peace-loving than some other tradition is to undermine one's original intention. Living nonviolently calls for humility and mutual understanding, whereas self-righteousness makes nonviolence virtually impossible. As we investigate this subject historically and personally, it helps to bear in mind how often we fall short of embodying our own ideals.

In this essay I have chosen to focus on four Theravada Buddhist figures, past and present, who are regarded as exemplars of nonviolent living. Nonviolence is a way of being in the world, not some kind of intellectual exercise. When it comes to religious ethics, exemplary behavior is a more potent guiding and motivating force than abstract principles. Thus Gandhi changed the course of history more through his nonviolent actions than by what he said or wrote about nonviolence. And Martin Luther King shook the foundations of racial discrimination in the United States not just by talking about brotherly love and human dignity, but by putting such principles into practice.

What we learn of nonviolence from Theravada sources has much in common with the other major branches of the Buddhist tradition. The precept against taking life, from the monastic code of conduct (Vinaya) written in Pali, is certainly the cardinal precept of all Buddhist schools. Likewise, the central Theravadin concept of nonself (*anattā*) must figure prominently in any Buddhist philosophy of nonviolence. The heroic accomplishments of Aśoka, the Buddhist ruler who renounced the use of violence, are recognized not only in the Pali chronicles but throughout the canonical literature of Buddhism. The same can be said about the states of other-regarding consciousness cultivated by Theravadins: for example, equanimity (*upekkhā*) is prized by Buddhists everywhere as a consummate expression of nonviolence. In its essentials, the Dhamma of Theravada Buddhism is the selfsame Dharma of Mahayana Buddhism—both terms refer simultaneously to the Buddha's teachings and the highest truth.

The Pali texts underscore restraint and generosity as two essential aspects of nonviolent living. Restraint means to curb the pursuit of self-interest or self-aggrandizement, out of respect for the interests of others. Generosity, the complement of restraint, is the active furthering of the total well-being of others. While these two virtues hardly exhaust the nature of nonviolence, no Buddhist approach to nonviolence can exclude them. Countless stories from the Theravada tradition illustrate the interplay between restraint and generosity and also point to a higher goal—the transformed state of being that accompanies a life of selflessness.

King Aśoka

After Shakyamuni himself, the first notable examplar of nonviolence in Theravada Buddhism is King Aśoka, who ruled the North Indian kingdom of Magadha from 272 to 236 B.C.E.[1] According to traditional sources, in the ninth year of Aśoka's reign a war broke out between Magadha and Kaliṅga, the most powerful North Indian state independent of Aśoka's rule. Magadha was victorious, but the horrors that accompanied the conquest were more than King Aśoka could bear. Much of what we know about Aśoka was originally inscribed in stone, because he commissioned rock and pillar edicts to tell his own story and promulgate his laws. The Thirteenth Rock Edict states that the war caused such bloodshed, disease, and dislocation of noncombatants that deep feelings of pity and remorse were aroused in the King's mind. As a result, he had a conversion experience in which he embraced Buddhism and renounced all further violence. He came to realize that genuine conquest cannot be achieved by force of arms but only by the power of truth and justice.

The story of Aśoka, like many accounts of conversion, falls into two contrasting parts. The King saw the first half of his life as one of heedlessness, hedonism, and rapacious aggression. Indeed, in the early part of his life he was so cruel that he acquired the epithet Aśoka the Blackguard (Canda-aśoka). After his conversion he became Dhamma-aśoka, the embodiment of righteousness and order. As an evil king, Aśoka had previously taken pleasure excursions, during which he hunted and indulged in other hurtful pastimes; as a benevolent monarch, he now embarked on Dhamma tours (*Dhamma-yattas*), during which he established hospitals, visited centers for the elderly, ministered to the needs of rural folk, and taught the Dhamma (Rock Edict VIII). Where he had once ruled by violence, he now promulgated laws promoting nonviolence. These not only proscribed the taking of life; they also encouraged respect toward all forms of sentient existence and nature in general. Recognizing that a truly nonviolent way of life could not be realized by legislation alone, he further urged his people to attain insight through meditation. In an edict that is often cited, the King declared:

> People can be induced to advance in the Dhamma by only two means, namely moral prescriptions and meditation. Of the two, moral prescriptions are the lesser, meditation the greater. The moral prescriptions I have promulgated include rules making certain animals inviolable, and I have established many other rules as well. But even in the case of abstention from injuring and killing living creatures, it is by meditation that people have made the greatest progress in the Dhamma.[2]

Aśoka's life (at least as depicted in the edicts and chronicles) exemplifies a nonviolent way of being in the world, based on the restraint of egoistic impulses and the generous expression of concern for others. Through his leadership, a kingdom that had once been governed according to power and privilege was transformed into a humanitarian welfare state. As interpreted by Aśoka, Buddhist Dhamma thus embraced a wide range of personal and sociopolitical goals: economy in expenditures, avoidance of disputes, gentleness toward parents, liberality toward friends, self-mastery, purity of heart, gratitude, and fidelity (Rock Edicts III, VII).

Aśoka's impact was so great that he came to be depicted in the Pali chronicles as an embodiment of the mythic *cakkavatti*, or universal monarch.[3] Such a ruler restores order and harmony to a world thrown into social chaos by greed and egotism. He protects all beings, rules with justice and impartiality, loves princes and ordinary subjects equally, and heeds the instructions of his religious advisors. A Righteous King of Truth was said to manifest ten royal virtues: generosity, morality, liberality, uprightness, gentleness, self-restraint, nonanger, nonviolence, forebearance, and nonopposition. The historical Aśoka was credited with all of these attributes, and he engendered an ideal that inspired emulation throughout the Buddhist world. Aniruddha of Pagan (eleventh century) and Tilokaraja of Chiang Mai (fifteenth century) are two notable examples of rulers who sought to model themselves after their illustrious Indian predecessor. Even if one discounts the extravagant praise heaped upon Aśoka by later generations, it is clear from the rock edicts and other historical evidence that he seriously explored the application of Buddhist tenets in the social realm. His efforts remain relevant today for anyone interested in organizing a state according to nonviolent principles.

Prince Vessantara

Countless Theravadin stories and legends illustrate further dimensions of nonviolent living. Though certain aspects of these tales are undoubtedly strange to modern ears, we must recall their didactic function: to convey their moral lessons as vividly and memorably as possible.

In Theravada countries the story of Prince Vessantara is second in popularity only to the story of the Buddha. Vessantara was the son of Sanjaya, King of Sivi.[4] Rather than indulging himself in his privileges, the Prince delighted in giving away anything that he happened to acquire. One day, however, he went too far. Graciously acceding to a request by eight Brahmans from a neighboring kingdom, he presented them with the King's white elephant, which had magical rain-making powers. The people of the country were outraged, and they forced the King to expel his son to a distant forest. Before Vessantara left, he gave away most of his personal possessions; all that remained was his wife Maddi, his two children, a chariot, and eight horses. As this modest entourage was leaving the city, someone asked Vessantara if he could spare his horses and his chariot, so he promptly gave them away too.

Proceeding on foot, the Prince and his family finally reached their destination deep in the forest. They erected a humble dwelling and lived together happily for about four months. One day a greedy old Brahman named Jujaka arrived, and he told Vessantara that he needed the Prince's children in his own household, as servants for his young wife. Despite the pain of separation from his beloved son and daughter, Vessantara consented. Finally, the god Indra disguised himself as a human being and appealed to Vessantara to surrender Maddi, his last and greatest treasure. In agreeing even to this request, Vessantara proved the ultimate depth of his self-giving nature. He was then rewarded by the gods, receiving back manyfold all that he had generously surrendered.

The traditional story is not concerned with a number of complexities that we might perceive in Vessantara's actions. For instance, there is no consideration of the feelings of the wife or children who are being given away. Nor is there any assessment of the relative merits of two noble ideals that sometimes come into conflict: generosity toward strangers versus love for particular individuals. But the story has been told and retold for centuries because it represents the Buddhist ideal of generosity, or *dāna*. Vessantara did not perform acts of charity in order to gain a reward; they were simply a natural expression of his selfless character. For Buddhists, the generosity that arises from selflessness is one of the essential meanings of nonviolence, not as an abstract principle but as a way of being in the world.

The Merchant Jotika

Another well-known story that recounts the impact of restraint and generosity is found in a fourteenth-century Pali text attributed to a great Thai monarch.[5] In this case the hero is a merchant named Jotika, who is said to have lived in the city of Rajagaha (Skt. Rajagriha) at the time of the Buddha. Jotika was fabulously wealthy. His seven-story mansion was decorated with seven precious gems, surrounded by seven jewel-studded walls, and augmented by four boundless treasuries of gold, silver, and additional gems. The merchant's virtuous wife possessed an equally miraculous rice pot that never became empty. Everyone knew about the couple's good fortune. The people who came from all over Jambu-dīpa (greater India) to admire Jotika's mansion were fed generously and given jewels from the wish-fulfilling trees that grew in the garden. Bimbisara, King of Rajagaha, understood that Jotika's wealth was a result of the great spiritual merit that the merchant had accumulated in previous lives. When the King visited Jotika, he was regaled with a feast of the most delicious food he had ever eaten. The King's entire retinue was fed from a single pot of rice and curry, which remained full no matter how much was taken from it. Bimbisara respectfully gave Jotika a white tiered umbrella, and Jotika gave the King a *manirattana* gem so brilliant that it burned like an eternal flame.

But not everyone was so kindly disposed toward the prosperous merchant. The King's son Ajatasattu conspired to kill his father, assume the throne, and seize Jotika's property. He struck on an *uposatha* day, when it is the custom of laypeople to observe eight of the ten precepts upheld by monks and nuns. While Jotika was at the monastery listening to the Dhamma, the traitorous Ajatasattu surrounded the seven-story mansion with an army. But the attackers were driven off by Jotika's courageous guards, and Ajatasattu was forced to flee through the city. Suddenly Ajatasattu came upon Jotika, who quickly surmised what had happened.

The upright Jotika patiently explained that since his wealth had been earned through merit, it could not be taken from him by force. It could, however, be given away. To demonstrate his point, he told Ajatasattu to try to remove the twenty rings that adorned his fingers, but they would not budge. Yet when Jotika lowered his arms, the rings slipped right off his fingers onto the ground. What Jotika did next is regarded as the climax of the story: he announced that he would become a monk and transfer all his merit to Ajatasattu. The traitorous Prince assumed that he would now be able to acquire Jotika's wealth, and he was delighted. However, the moment the devout householder was ordained as a monk, all of his property sank into the ground, gone forever. By the end of the story, Jotika attains the status of an *arahant*, the highest stage of moral and spiritual self-realization. And Ajatasattu eventually becomes a follower of the Buddha and a supporter of the monastic order.

Several aspects of this account may raise questions for contemporary readers. If the story is meant to extol renunciation, why is Jotika's great wealth understood to be a result of spiritual merit? When Jotika announced his plan to join the order, was he intent on inspiring Ajatasattu by demonstrating his own nonattachment, or did the transfer of merit also constitute a practical form of assistance? Doesn't the notion that spiritual merit can be "transferred" (an idea usually associated with Mahayana Buddhism) abrogate the orderly workings of karma? Does the apparently spontaneous disappearance of Jotika's riches upon his ordination contradict his earlier claim that he could give his wealth away? As some of these questions suggest, it is not entirely clear how Jotika's becoming a monk and renouncing his wealth/merit served to benefit Ajatasattu.

Traditional interpretations of the tale do not linger over these fine points, however. In Theravada Buddhism the story of Jotika, like the story of Vessantara, teaches the proper attitude of nonattachment toward all material possessions. In both accounts, the wealth is merit-earned, and the two moral exemplars are entirely free from attachment to it. As a result, their generosity is unqualified and inexhaustible. Jotika's act of renunciation (a definitive expression of self-restraint) is simultaneously a consummate expression of generosity. The Buddhist view is that the two are inseparable: generosity always implies restraint, and restraint always implies generosity.

Acharn Buddhadasa

When we shift our attention from the classical tradition to the present, we again find many exemplars of a nonviolent, socially transformational mode of life. Among laypeople, notable contributions have recently been made by A. T. Ariyaratne, the founder of the Sarvodaya Shramadana movement in Sri Lanka, and by our fellow contributor Sulak Sivaraksa, who cofounded the Asian Cultural Forum on Development and the Thai Inter-Religious Commission for Development. Among monks, a contemporary figure who has achieved international stature is the Thai master Acharn Buddhadasa. (*Acharn* is the Thai version of the Pali *ācariya*, or teacher.) Buddhadasa recently celebrated not only his eighty-fourth birthday but also over sixty years as a monk and over half a century as the abbot of Suan Mokh, a forest monastery in southern Thailand. His life and teachings have important implications for our consideration of Buddhism and nonviolence.[6]

Buddhadasa was born in 1906 in the district of Chaiya, southern Thailand. He was ordained as a monk in 1926. After six years of monastic study spent largely in Bangkok, he withdrew to an overgrown, abandoned monastery near his hometown, renaming it Suan Mokh (Garden of Empowering Liberation). Buddhadasa has never been an "ordinary" monk. He has eschewed more conventional monastic roles and the trappings of ecclesiastical office in order to pursue a life he considers closer to the Buddha's Dhamma. At the same time, his reformist teachings reflect various modern trends in Buddhist thought, and they address the dramatic social changes that Thailand has experienced since the overthrow of monarchical rule in 1932.[7]

Although Buddhadasa and Suan Mokh embody the peaceful, nonacquisitive ideals of early Buddhism, they have had an unparalleled impact on contemporary Thai Buddhism. Monastic dwellings at Suan Mokh retain the rustic simplicity of early Buddhist forest shelters, yet the compound also includes a "spiritual theater" that utilizes the latest audio-visual technology to teach the fundamentals of Buddhism. Buddhadasa himself wears mismatched cast-off robes, and he has steadfastly refused to become embroiled in the politics of the national Thai Sangha. Nonetheless, his controversial interpretations of Buddha-dhamma have aroused and sustained the interest of many Buddhist leaders and intellectuals in Thailand and abroad. Suan Mokh, though far removed from any major city, annually attracts thousands of foreign visitors for study and meditation.

Buddhadasa's place in Thai Buddhism is assured, but the nature and extent of his contribution will be a matter of continuing study for years to come. Like many original thinkers, he has aroused opposition at different points in his career. He has been criticized by meditation practitioners for the prolixity of his writings, by traditional Abhidhammists for the unorthodoxy of his thought, and by political activists for the idealism of his approach to society. Because Buddhadasa has chosen to teach in a remote forest setting, far from the complexities of modern urban life, the critics of his political approach have mistakenly assumed that he advocates an otherworldly kind of Buddhism, one that focuses on personal transformation to the exclusion of social change.

To be sure, Buddhadasa emphasizes the importance of right view and correct practice on the individual level. But Suan Mokh also represents a model community rather than a place for individuals to retreat from the world. Monks and nuns, laymen and laywomen, the young and the elderly, as well as many kinds of animals and plants live together there in a spirit of harmony. At daybreak Buddhadasa can usually be found teaching under the trees surrounded by attentive human listeners, scratching dogs, and crowing roosters. Orange-robed monks sitting motionless on benches and tree stumps seem part of the natural landscape in the predawn light. Suan Mokh is an attempt to actualize a balanced state of nature (*dhammajāti*), which should not be confused with a regression to primitivity. It is a setting which enables people to act out of mutual concern and respect for the good of the larger group. Such a community illustrates a cornerstone of Buddhadasa's thought, an ideal that he calls dhammic socialism (*dhammika sangha-niyama*).

Buddhadasa's point of view is grounded in fundamental Buddhist tenets, particularly the principle of overcoming attachment to self, to "me" and "mine." Thus he asserts that personal and social well-being depend upon the transformation of self-interest into selflessness and concern for others. The ideal society that he envisions is based on a deep appreciation of the equality of all beings. Rather than attempting to erase differences, such a society seeks to accommodate individual variation by recognizing that everyone, regardless of position, has a place of dignity within the community. Buddhadasa's view of a just and nonviolent society coincides with his notion of the original state of nature—a condition of mutual interdependence, balance, and selflessness. This state is also the basic nature of human beings, as realized through enlightenment. Because this primordial selflessness has been lost, we live in bondage to delusion, attachment, and unquenchable craving. We then respond to our confusion and suffering by developing even more attachment and craving.

How can we break such a vicious cycle? Here Buddhadasa again embraces time-honored Theravada teachings. On the personal level, the methods of mindfulness (*sati*), continuous full attention (*sampajañña*), and focused concentration (*samādhi*) are the best way to overturn greed, ignorance, and egoism. On the social level, we cannot expect everyone to become enlightened, but even a slight attitudinal shift in favor of selflessness and harmony can facilitate many positive changes, whether the arena is local or international. Buddhadasa believes that it is not unrealistic to require people in positions of power to promote policies that not only meet the basic needs of all, but that also address spiritual concerns holistically.

Buddhadasa does not endorse capitalism or communism, "individualist democracy" or "violent proletarian revolution." He concedes that the ideal of freedom associated with liberal democracy is attractive, but he believes that its ambiguity promotes the notion that anything one wants to do is acceptable. Human greed and other defilements are so strong that they run amuck in a democratic capitalist system: self-centeredness reigns, the weak are exploited, and certain people are allowed to accumulate vast wealth. Though classic forms of socialism may appear less acquisitive and less competitive than capitalism, in Buddhadasa's view "so-called socialism" also succumbs to materialism and combativeness.

Buddhadasa's Dhammic Socialism

Attempting to articulate his own vision of a Buddhistic socialism, Buddhadasa begins with simple definitions and homespun illustrations. To him, socialism means "not taking more than one's fair share—using only what is necessary so that the rest is available for others."[8] In an earlier era, he explains, farmers who were cultivating fields or rice paddies willingly made allowances for the produce that would be eaten by stray animals or taken by hungry people. As they worked, they recited a verse:

> Food for a hungry bird is our merit;
> Food for a hungry person—our charity.[9]

When Buddhadasa considers the sociopolitical implications of Buddhism, he finds it to be inherently socialistic, at least according to his own conception of that term. A monk was not allowed to use four pieces of cloth to make his robe, because it could be done with three; nor could he own more than a single bowl, because he could feed himself adequately with just one. According to Buddhadasa's reading of original Buddhism, the welfare of the community took precedence, and self-restraint followed as a matter of course. Thus he asserts:

> If we hold fast to Buddhism we shall have a socialist disposition in our flesh and blood. We shall see our fellow humans as friends in suffering—in birth, old age, sickness, and death—and hence we cannot abandon them. . . . This is the ideal of pure socialism which must be acted out, not just talked about for political purposes or for selfish, devious gain.[10]

The straightforward quality of Buddhadasa's socialism allows him to call all other religions socialist as well: "The founders of every religion have wanted people to live according to socialist principles in order to act in the interest of society as a whole."[11] In other words, overcoming attachment to self is the heart of all religions and the prerequisite for acting on behalf of others.

Buddhadasa's dhammic socialism can also be discussed in terms of three basic principles: the good of the whole, restraint, and respect for life. In the world he envisions, the first principle informs political, economic, and social structures; the second governs individual behavior; and the third prescribes the correct attitude toward all forms of existence. For Buddhadasa, the principle of the good of the whole is applicable on micro and macro levels alike. Just as the body is unhealthy if its various parts are not working in concert, the well-being of a particular village depends upon the cooperation of the villagers and, on a larger scale, upon the cooperation between villages. Indeed, "the entire universe is a socialist system. Countless numbers of stars in the sky exist together in a socialist system."[12] Since this is the way of nature, it is also proper for human beings to be steadfast in recognizing the good of the whole and acting accordingly.

From an awareness of interdependence follows the second principle, restraint (and its corollary, generosity). Buddhadasa believes that an earlier age was more aware than ours of the way in which everything exists together in a unity:

> Our ancestors knew this. Thus they taught that we should do what we can to promote the coexistence of all beings, and that we should be kind to one another according to the law of nature. All living beings are able to exist to the degree that they form a society, a mutually beneficial cooperative. This is the handiwork of nature. If nature lacked this character, we would all die. Those who know this principle hold fast to it.[13]

Dhammic socialism dictates a lifestyle of simplicity and moderation. While it recognizes that what counts as moderation or excess may vary among individuals, groups, and cultures, it still regards this principle as universally applicable. As a Buddhist monk, Buddhadasa finds the example of the Buddha and the traditional monastic way of life to be particularly instructive, though he does not suggest that everyone should become a monk or a nun. Each person must work out his or her own "middle way" between the extremes of self-indulgence and austerity.

The principle of restraint should be understood as optimizing rather than limiting human freedom. The "freedom" of liberal democracy, Buddhadasa argues, tends to isolate the good of the individual from that of the group, placing the two in conflict. In dhammic socialism, however, freedom is seen in the context of interrelational matrices reaching from the level of atoms to the cosmos as a whole. The individual feels part of this incalculably vast network that nevertheless expresses itself in the details of each person's situation. When the good of the individual is recognized as inseparable from the good of the whole, human freedom acquires a much grander meaning than the mere absence of restriction.

Buddhadasa's third principle of dhammic socialism—respect for life—again posits a universe in which everyone and everything is interdependent. Naturally, this principle upholds peace and nonviolence:

> Today people are so cruel that they have dropped a bomb knowing that it could kill thousands of human beings. Our ancestors would have surrendered before committing such a horrendous act. So-called socialist as well as capitalist countries are prepared to drop such bombs. . . . If we want peace we should choose the path of peace. Killing others will only lead to being killed. The only way of living harmoniously together is to act out of loving-kindness.[14]

Through its valuation of all living things, the principle of respect for life also provides a vantage point from which to criticize the ecological threat posed by our technological, industrialized society.

Buddhadasa goes on to assert that Buddhism has much to contribute to building a peaceful, nonviolent world. In a recent lecture commemorating the Buddha's first discourse, he outlined some of the qualities that would make one a Buddhist peacemaker. Such a person should: (1) be educated not only intellectually but also morally; (2) be healthy physically (not self-indulgent), mentally (free from mental defilements), and spiritually (free from false conceptions and blind faith); (3) realize his or her responsibilities toward others; (4) live moderately and be generous to those in need; (5) practice the Dhamma for the sake of the Dhamma and not with any hope of reward; (6) promote the moral conditions that reflect the proper balance and harmony of life; (7) recognize the essential connection between right knowledge and right action; and (8) lead a "cool" (nirvanic) life.[15] As he repeatedly reminds his listeners: "The role of religion is to solve our basic human problems in order to bring about peace, to put an end to turmoil and confusion."[16]

While many of Buddhadasa's teachings seem to have universal application, others address the situation that he and his countrymen face in present-day Thailand. If a forest fire is raging, he explains metaphorically, one may have to protect oneself by scorching the area around one's own house. In a world inflamed by greedy capitalism and violent socialism, the best course for Thailand may be a "dictatorial" dhammic socialism. By dictatorial, Buddhadasa means a benevolent form of centralized authority capable of making decisions swiftly, for the benefit of the whole. Thus he is well disposed toward enlightened kingship (monarchy and Buddhism have long coexisted in Thailand). He argues:

> A ruler who embodies the ten royal virtues will be the best kind of socialist dictator. This way of thinking will be totally foreign to most Westerners who are unfamiliar with this kind of Buddhist kingly rule. . . . Because we misunderstand the meaning of kingship, we consider all monarchical systems wrong.[17]

In this connection, Buddhadasa notes that the world *rāja*, now rendered only as "king," originally meant "contentment"—because a leader's primary responsibility is the contentment of the entire community.

Certain elements in Buddhadasa's teachings are vulnerable to criticism. Those accustomed to the intellectual rigor of Western philosophy may find Buddhadasa's statements too general, his definitions too loose, and his arguments too unsystematic. Even sympathetic observers have suggested that he is overly eager to identify similarities between Buddhism and quite diverse ways of thinking.[18] Claims such as the following might strike anthropologists and others as simplistic:

> Even the earliest humans had no social problems as we have today, because they had not begun to hoard resources. They lived according to a natural socialism for hundreds of thousands of years.[19]

Buddhadasa's accomplishments are nonetheless considerable. Whereas Asian political leaders like Mao drew inspiration from Marx, and Buddhist statesmen like Bandaranaike relied heavily upon Western political theory, Buddhadasa has taken an Asian belief-system and used it to create a contemporary political philosophy that accords with its Asian setting. Certain criticisms of his work require qualification. For instance, most of Buddhadasa's writings have been transcribed from taped lectures, and they retain the spontaneous, "unsystematic" character of the original lecture format. Buddhadasa's intention is not to develop a coherent philosophy—indeed he sharply criticizes "philosophizing"—so it may not be appropriate to judge his thought along those lines. Moreover, Buddhadasa's teachings are grounded in the Buddhist belief that without right understanding there cannot be right action. Rather than trying to disseminate doctrines in a conventional sense, he strives to provoke insights that will transform people's lives and inspire them to build a better world.

As the post-Cold War world extricates itself from the constant threat of nuclear holocaust, a model such as Suan Mokh may suggest new possibilities for actualizing a nonviolent way of life. While Buddhadasa's vision may be utopian, it is not otherworldly. He has outlined the basic principles of a political/spiritual philosophy that has the potential not only to influence Thailand, but to guide all nations struggling to create an equitable and peaceful society. Buddhadasa's teachings reflect a wide range of voices—Asian and Western, Buddhist and non-Buddhist. His Dhamma is an expression of a uniquely creative mind and a singular life story.

King Aśoka, a historical figure whose life acquired mythic proportions, demonstrates that a country can be ruled nonviolently by an enlightened and compassionate leader. Vessantara, a legendary prince who gave away everything, symbolizes the unconditional generosity that characterizes a person grounded in nonviolence. The merchant Jotika, in another fabulous tale, renounced all his wealth to become a monk, thereby manifesting the self-restraint inherent in a nonviolent lifestyle. Acharn Buddhadasa, a contemporary Thai master, exposes further dimensions of nonviolence in his teachings, in the community that has grown up around him, and in the way that he leads his life. However remote in time or place these exemplars may appear, they offer us abundant hints for making our own lives more nonviolent, "cool," and nirvanic. As Buddhadasa concludes, "If all beings have 'cooled' lives, the whole world will be in peace."[20]

Notes

1. For a closely related discussion of Aśoka, see Donald K. Swearer, *Buddhism and Society in Southeast Asia* (Chambersburg, PA: Anima Books, 1980), 46ff. A seminal account of Aśoka's life is presented in John S. Strong, *The Legend of King Aśoka: A Study and Translation of the Aśokavadana* (Princeton: Princeton University Press, 1983).
2. N. A. Nikam and Richard McKeon, trans., *The Edicts of Aśoka* (Chicago: University of Chicago Press, 1959), 40 (modified slightly).
3. The qualities of the universal monarch are described in the *Cakkavatti Sīhanāda Suttānta* and the *Aggañña Suttānta*, both in the *Dīgha Nikāya*.
4. The legend of Vessantara is found in the *Dāsajātaka*, the last ten of the canonical stories of the previous lives of the Buddha.
5. This text, the *Trai Bhumi Phra Ruang*, has been translated by Frank E. Reynolds and Mani B. Reynolds as *The Three Worlds of King Ruang* (Berkeley: Asian Humanities Press, 1982). For the story of Jotika, see 189–200.

6. Portions of this discussion are adapted from the introduction to Buddhadasa, *Me and Mine: Selected Essays of Bhikkhu Buddhadasa*, edited by Donald K. Swearer (Albany: State University of New York Press, 1989). The essays on dhammic socialism in that volume are revised and reprinted from Buddhadasa, *Dhammic Socialism*, edited by Donald K. Swearer (Bangkok: Thai Inter-Religious Commission for Development, 1986).

7. For a discussion of Buddhadasa's context, see Peter A. Jackson, *Buddhadasa: A Buddhist Thinker for the Modern World* (Bangkok: The Siam Society, 1988), especially the introduction and first two chapters.

8. Buddhadasa, "Democratic Socialism," in *Me and Mine*, 172.

9. Ibid., 178.

10. Buddhadasa, "A Socialism Capable of Benefitting the World," in *Me and Mine*, 195.

11. Buddhadasa, "Democratic Socialism," in *Me and Mine*, 172.

12. Buddhadasa, "A Socialism Capable of Benefitting the World," in *Me and Mine*, 200.

13. Ibid., 196 (with slight alterations in translation).

14. Ibid., 199.

15. Buddhadasa, "Till the World Is with Peace," in *Me and Mine*, 204–206.

16. Buddhadasa, "Democratic Socialism," in *Me and Mine*, 170.

17. Buddhadasa, "A Dictatorial Dhammic Socialism," in *Me and Mine*, 192.

18. Robert Bobilin, *Revolution from Below: Buddhist and Christian Movements for Justice in Asia* (Lanham, Md.: University Press of America, 1988), 90.

19. Buddhadasa, "A Dictatorial Dhammic Socialism," in *Me and Mine*, 187.

20. Buddhadasa, "Till the World Is with Peace," in *Me and Mine*, 206.

5

Tibet and the Monastic Army of Peace

by Robert A. F. Thurman

According to an old Tibetan tradition, the bodhisattva Avalokiteśvara has a special relation with the people of Tibet. A bodhisattva is a warrior or hero of enlightenment, a being who is on the path to buddhahood. But in a sense, Avalokiteśvara is even more than a buddha. After attaining buddhahood, he voluntarily returned to the way of a bodhisattva in order to lead all beings to buddhahood. Thus Avalokiteśvara is considered the manifestation of the selfless, unconditional compassion of the buddhas.

The form of Avalokiteśvara favored by the Tibetans has a thousand arms, a thousand eyes (in his open palms), and eleven heads. He is said to have acquired these many arms and heads as a result of his frustration with the Tibetans. The story begins when Avalokiteśvara was dwelling in Sukhāvatī, the Pure Land of Amitābha Buddha, where everything was wonderfully peaceful. Feeling quite confident and expansive, Avalokiteśvara decided to go down to Tibet to help it become a civilized, nonviolent nation. He vowed to Amitābha: "If I should ever get discouraged down there, working with those barbaric Tibetans, may my body he shattered into a thousand pieces." Then he descended, and for several lifetimes he meditated in the mountains upon boundless compassion, continually emanating waves of love.

In those days the Tibetans were powerful warriors who had conquered much of Central Asia. They also loved to have a good time and eat great quantities of yak meat. In the traditional language of Buddhism, they were difficult to tame. After many lifetimes, Avalokiteśvara began to be aware that such deeply ingrained tendencies are not easily pacified. Just emanating waves of love does not do the trick—violence somehow persists. Offer food to a hungry demon, and he responds by starting to eat your arm. In a moment when Avalokiteśvara was not guarding his mind, he thought: "These evil, violent Tibetans are insatiable. No matter how peaceful and loving I am, it has no effect." He became a bit discouraged and wept, they say, two tears. From each tear a goddess was born, one white and one green— the two forms of Tārā. The two goddesses said, "Stop worrying, we'll help you. Please calm yourself." And their words indeed calmed him down for a lifetime or two. At last, however, he became truly discouraged, and in that moment his body was instantly shattered to bits.

Then one of the fragments of the bodhisattva cried out in despair to Amitābha Buddha for help. Amitābha came down to the place where Avalokiteśvara's pieces were strewn about the mountain. In typical guru fashion, he looked down at the broken bodhisattva and said, "What's your problem? Who ever told you take such an ambitious vow? What have you done to yourself? You know, you should always be careful about what you wish for, because—whatever it is, good or bad—sooner or later you will get it." Then Amitābha blessed the bodhisattva, and the thousand pieces became an imposing figure with a thousand arms, a thousand eyes, and eleven heads. The arms symbolize the power of a thousand world-conquering kings; the eyes symbolize the enlightened vision of a thousand buddhas. Ten of the heads stand for the ten stages of a bodhisattva's path to buddhahood.[1]

The eleventh and topmost head is the most interesting one in relation to nonviolence. It has a wrathful expression, capable of turning any manifestation of violence back upon itself. This depiction recognizes that nonviolence and compassion also have a certain fierce aspect. For example, in the *Bodhisattva-bhūmi*, a Buddhist text of the fourth century C.E., Asaṅga argues that a bodhisattva is compelled to kill someone if that is the only way he can save the life of many people, though killing violates a fundamental monastic and ethical precept. Yet even if he has to take life in order to save life, he does not do so aggressively. He acts with regret and love toward the person he must kill.[2] If we define violence as force used in connection with hatred, anger, or aggression, then the taking of life by the bodhisattva is not violence. However, if we do not include this motivational factor in the definition of violence and only consider the effect on others, then this act of the bodhisattva is indeed violence. Accordingly, it is the fiercely compassionate form of Avalokiteśvara, reconstituted from a thousand fragments, who is deemed truly competent to save beings from suffering, and he is regarded by the Tibetans as a kind of messiah.

The Significance of Tibet

Buddhism was transmitted to Tibet about a thousand years ago, as the religion's strength was ebbing in its Indian homeland. Because Tibet and India were separated only by a difficult journey through the Himalayan passes, Tibet's reception of the teachings, lineages, and institutions of Indian Buddhism was more complete than that of other Asian nations. Once the Buddha's teaching, or Dharma, was established in this isolated place, it flourished there undisturbed for a millennium. While the Buddhist traditions of other countries were disrupted by political turmoil or social developments, Tibet upheld and safeguarded the teaching for a future time.

A pattern developed in which the rulership of the country became a Buddhist institution: the roles of Buddhist monk and Buddhist king were unified in the person of the Dalai Lama. An essential part of this spiritual-temporal government was based on the notion of reincarnation. When an important leader died, a young boy would be identified as his reincarnation; then the boy would be trained to take over the predecessor's position. Such arrangements enabled Tibetan society to remain harmonious during the seventeenth, eighteenth, and nineteenth centuries. The main business of everyone was supposed to be enlightenment; those who felt they could not attain it in this lifetime were expected to support those who could, for the benefit of all.

The Tibetan ideal was the unity of Dharma and state, Dharma and society, Dharma and life. This might at first trouble us because of the American principle of the separation of church and state. Throughout history, religions have indeed been the cause of suffering for countless beings in many different situations. Wars, inquisitions, and intolerance of all kinds have been carried out in the name of religion. However, we need not equate the Dharma with this kind of religion and its dogmatic insistence on certain doctrines and institutions. Real religion is nothing but the energy to help sentient beings; all religions were originally founded to promote happiness and reduce suffering. If the Dharma is the liberating truth of enlightenment, the awareness of an inexpressible ultimate reality, then the potential of human life can best be fulfilled in a society that is one with the Dharma. What we desire most is a community in which everyone interacts selflessly. In such a nirvanic society no one would suffer from neglect, because many other people would be concerned about each individual's well-being.

Perhaps the Tibetans became too happy with their monk-king system, in the sense that they began to ignore the rest of the world. As the twentieth century approached, there were hardly any soldiers in Tibet, and the militarily defenseless country was easy prey—first for the British, then for the Communist Chinese. Since the forced occupation of Tibet by China in the early 1950s, the Tibetan people have truly suffered a holocaust. Over a million people have died. About three hundred thousand were killed through direct violence, including monks who were machine-gunned or beaten to death in the name of class struggle. The rest have died in famines caused by growing Chinese wheat instead of Tibetan barley, decimation of the animal population, and other disruptions of the ecology. By colonizing Tibet, China acquired a land mass nearly one-half the size of its own territory. The Chinese have plundered Tibet's natural resources and are now accused of dumping nuclear waste on the Tibetan plateau.

In accord with Communist policy, the Buddhist institution has been ruthlessly dismantled. The Dalai Lama was forced to flee his homeland in 1959. More than 6,000 monasteries were destroyed, libraries were set aflame, magnificent buddha images were blown up by hand grenades, and sacred stupas were bulldozed to the ground. This systematic devastation of one of the world's greatest Buddhist civilizations continues today.[3]

The conventional wisdom in the West regards Tibet as a lost cause, a hapless victim of geopolitical realities. Having seen certain imperfections in the Tibet of recent times, I too thought that Tibet's destruction was perhaps inevitable. In any case, it seemed to have fulfilled its mission to history—to bring us this marvelous Dharma that had been saved alive from ancient India, almost as in a time capsule. Moreover, very little could be done against that great leviathan, China.... Now, however, I have altered my outlook. No doubt inspired by the Tibetans' heroic and essentially nonviolent response to their plight, I believe that if human beings develop a certain positive will, they can succeed against any odds. If they do not visualize the evil that confronts them as invincible, then that evil actually loses much of its force. Militarism remains effective only as long as people are brainwashed into thinking that the militaristic approach is the best or last recourse available. In the same way, if nonviolence is to be powerful, the key to its strength must be people thinking it is powerful.

Thus in recent years I have come to see how significant it would be for China to free Tibet. Besides benefiting Tibet, it would also be a great service to the rest of the world—and especially to China. Such a move would be widely welcomed because it would be pragmatic and ethical at the same time. For not only have the Chinese been imposing an alien will on the Tibetan people, they have been unable to manage Tibet on a practical level. It would also be advantageous to allow a nation that has been living and breathing Buddha-dharma for a thousand years to have the opportunity to balance that experience with modernity. We would learn more from that interaction than we would from trying to reinvent the wheel ourselves.

The Tibetans feel—despite the suffering of their countrymen, the loss of their loved ones, and the loss of their homeland—that the ultimate meaning of human history has not been lost. They continue to believe that human life and history are not meaningless, that even the worst atrocities will eventually be redeemed through some kind of saving power from higher realms. These aspirations are often expressed in terms of the Kālachakra Buddha. Kālachakra literally means time machine or wheel of time. In the *Kālachakra Tantra*, there is a vision of history as an overall positive evolution on a planetary scale. The Kālachakra Buddha is completely capable of taking into account the entirety of such an evolutionary process and acting optimally for the benefit of the sentient beings who are part of it.[4]

Granted, such a positive view can be difficult to maintain. Buddhism itself lays great emphasis on suffering, and history has produced many human disasters on a massive scale. Sometimes people do die horribly; sometimes they kill or otherwise hideously malign each other. However, the vast perspective of the Kālachakra spans countless generations. According to this overall view, it is asserted that all human beings are evolving toward perfection, toward buddhahood, and that this evolution is actually following the best possible course.

The current Dalai Lama, who has been living in exile for over thirty years, maintains such a panoramic vision in his teachings. He tells his compatriots that whatever it was that brought misfortune upon them, their country, and their religion, their response must be a spiritual one, a nonviolent one. The Dalai Lama often speaks about the Chinese people and how much he owes them, how much the Tibetans have benefited by being tortured and driven out of their homeland. He feels that because of the Chinese, the Tibetans have learned a great deal about their own religious teaching, about suffering and impermanence, about homelessness, about compassion and tolerance. The Dalai Lama is himself considered to be an emanation of the Kālachakra Buddha, according to Vajrayana Buddhism. So the Tibetans believe that the Dalai Lama is staying in tune with the long-term processes of spiritual evolution, and that he is working toward the fulfillment of global history.

Buddhist Visions of Perfection

Besides the Kālachakra concept, there are other aspects of the Buddhist worldview that give the Tibetans solace and reinforce their faith in the eventual triumph of nonviolence. One of the fundamental teachings of Buddhism is that apparent reality is not ultimate reality. What is ultimately real is not the realm of suffering but the realm of immanent/transcendent perfection, which can be seen and experienced by those whose minds are unclouded. Numerous stories in the Mahayana sutras vividly express this cardinal tenet. For instance, the *Kāraṇḍavyūha Sūtra* describes Avalokiteśvara descending into a horrible hell. The tortured denizens there are continuously being plowed under with red-hot iron plows, exhumed, and plowed under again. In response, the compassionate bodhisattva directs water to flow from his thousand hands. The superheated iron land is cooled, the denizens' sufferings are ended, and the presiding devils run off. That region of hell is thereby emptied.[5]

A comparable idea is illustrated at greater length in the following incident from the *Vimilakīrti Sūtra*. Śāriputra, a leading disciple of the Buddha, had been taught that there are universes under the influence of particular buddhas, where all the residents are karmically connected in such a way as to contribute perfectly to each other's spiritual fruition. In these buddha-fields the precise balance conducive to enlightenment is present. Bliss and love are all-pervading, every action expresses selfless generosity, and nonviolence is fully actualized. There is surpassing beauty wherever one looks—jewels, lotuses, graceful waterfowl swimming on limpid pools. Having heard this, Śāriputra looked around him at the India of the fifth century B.C.E. and thought: "If a buddha-field is supposed to be so sublime and wonderful, reflecting the perfection of its buddha, how is it that this world I see around me resembles nothing so much as a pile of dung? Either Shakyamuni Buddha is a very imperfect buddha or what he has taught about buddha-fields is utter nonsense." Śāriputra of course didn't say anything like this out loud or reveal what he was actually thinking about his master. However, the Buddha had developed what all great spiritual teachers should have—clairvoyance concerning the inner workings of their disciples' minds. So, very embarrassingly for Śāriputra, the Buddha asked him:

"Śāriputra, what do you think? Is it the fault of the sun and moon that those blind from birth cannot see the sun or the moon?"

"Oh no, Buddha, it's not the fault of the sun and moon."

"Therefore, Śāriputra, it is not my fault that imperfect beings, their minds clogged by obscurations and dualistic consciousness, see my buddha-field as a world full of dung. That is not how it actually is, but that is how they see it." Then the Buddha said, "Śāriputra, I'll show you what I mean," and he touched the ground with his big toe. Instantly, Śāriputra and all the others present saw the world around them as a perfect environment. They saw their own bodies as made of pure, jewel-like, living plasma. They saw themselves seated on gorgeous lotuses, weightlessly afloat in equipoise. Everything was in a transparent state of mutual interpenetration, a cosmic harmony optimally conducive to universal liberation.

"How is it?" said the Buddha.

"Oh, wonderful!"

Everyone was absorbed in the delight of this vision. Then the Buddha lifted his foot, and everything again looked just as it had before—the usual world of dualism and problems.[6] This little drama, coming near the beginning of the sutra, poses a central question that runs through the rest of the text: If the world is so perfect and there are beings who have the ability to actualize this perfection, then why are things left like this? Buddhism holds that this apparent dilemma is capable of genuine resolution, to be experienced rather than conceptualized.

Another variation on these themes is the concept of a golden age yet to come, sometimes identified by the Tibetans as the future kingdom of Shambhala. At such a time, divine energy will pervade everything, and nonviolence will finally prevail. Instead of the good being oppressed by power, good and power will be one. Individual and society will no longer be in conflict, but will come to fruition together. In the spirit of Mahayana Buddhism, the Tibetans do not expect to be able to attain the complete perfection of a golden age until the entire world does so in unison.

Are these visions the Buddhist equivalent of Candide's best of all possible worlds? Are they another version of the inveterate theistic rationalization that everything is part of God's plan? Though there are similarities here to such views, there are also key differences. In Buddhism, higher beings are not able to save others simply by external means, because these higher beings did not create the world. No one created the world, which has neither beginning nor end. Buddhism teaches that beings have engendered their own problems from beginningless time, in accord with karma, or the law of cause and effect. Karma cannot simply be cancelled or set aside. Rather, we must learn to solve our own problems and to uproot the delusive tendencies that keep producing negative karma. Descriptions of buddha-fields make the point that whatever our predicament may be, we have all that we need to achieve spiritual liberation. Moreover, the most powerful forces—of enlightenment, compassion, nonviolence—are working on our behalf. Thus the Tibetans, even in the midst of terrible adversity, are nonetheless able to acknowledge the basic rightness of their situation.

The Monastic Strategy of Nonviolence

Americans, and modern people in general, are often afflicted with what I call temporal chauvinism—the assumption that anything devised or conceived before 1960 is primitive and useless. Let us say that today's temporal chauvinists suddenly have a clear vision of the frightful consequences of a nuclear war or accident. In fact, *we* might be the ones who get hit by the big bang. Thus we should do a great thing and figure out how to transmute the world into a state of nonviolence. It is assumed that no one in the past has tackled this problem with any degree of success. As for Buddhist monks wandering around in poor Third World countries, the usual reaction is: "Never mind them, their countries are in such bad shape they couldn't possibly have thought of anything."

Those who draw such conclusions are overlooking the nonviolent strategy and social policy instituted by Shakyamuni Buddha. The Buddhist monastic Sangha is a true army of nonviolence, one that has been at work on this planet for 2,500 years. Perhaps lay Buddhists are also part of this army, but the shock troops, the elite corps, have been the monks and nuns.

Although it is not usual to think of monasticism in terms of an army, for Buddhist monasticism the military metaphor is apt. People often have a romantic image of Shakyamuni as a pure spiritual person with no worldly concerns or know-how. Actually, Shakyamuni was trained to be a general. He went to the Shakya state's equivalent of West Point. The Indian kingdoms of his time were similar to the ancient Greek city-states, battling one another to see which one could create an empire. The kings were classed as *kṣatriya* (warriors), and they had to know how to manage armies. Shakyamuni was educated as a future king until his thirtieth year, so he was not naive about the exercise of power. In fact, he was a professional in these matters.

But then the well-trained prince renounced his profession. He went through an intense personal voyage and discovered the true nature of the self, which is selflessness. He realized that on the basis of selflessness human life is extremely workable, just as it is totally unworkable on the basis of selfhood. Paradoxical as it may seem, selflessness functions as the wellspring of creative individuality and as the source of an outward-directed dynamism. In light of these insights, the situation on our planet looked quite promising to Shakyamuni. But then he also had to take into consideration all the kings and their ministers who were fixated on killing each other, whose violent habit patterns were deeply entrenched. His fellow Indians were especially fierce—their descendants defeated Alexander the Great, rather savagely.

So Shakyamuni began to consider how people could be tamed. He may have thought something like this: "One individual taming his own mind is good, but what is needed is millions of individuals helping millions of others tame their minds. And this process of taming has to be able to go on in the midst of many other people behaving violently, even killing those who have been tamed. What can be done? We will have to create an army. Since these kings are all drafting people into armies, we will make an army too. Our army will be an army of nonviolent warriors, whose battle will be to conquer the self. Like regular soldiers, they should be prepared to die for their cause. This is the best way to overthrow King Ignorance, Minister Lust, and Minister Hate, who rule the mind. What uniforms should our soldiers have? They should wear orange robes and shave their heads so they won't breed lice, just as regular soldiers living in barracks do. And they should take certain vows. . . ." In this way, the Buddha devised a kind of boot camp for training monks and, later, nuns. Buddhist activism began when the Buddha decided, "No, I will not run a kingdom. Instead, I'm going to start a Sangha, a monastic army."

In our culture and in earlier periods of world history, monasticism has generally been misunderstood and resisted. Present-day activists interested in promoting peace tend to see monasticism as introverted, selfish, and useless in terms of getting things done. Ideas and movements that go against the dominant utilitarian view of human life always encounter such resistance. In ancient times, Socrates was condemned for trying to teach a few young men in the bathhouse some things about philosophy that might have made them hesitate to fight the Spartans. Confucius was never given a permanent position by a Chinese ruler, in part because his teachings were thought to be sapping the martial vigor of the young Chinese nobles.

Yet the Buddha was remarkably successful. He would enter an Indian town and announce that anyone who joined his wandering flock of orange-robed mendicants would thereby be excused from taxes, family duties, social obligations, and military service. The organization that began this way quickly multiplied into the hundreds of thousands. It is astonishing that the Sangha was able to succeed in so many nations, even though rulers are quick to understand that a monastic army is a powerful counterforce to the state's militaristic aims. If people are monks and nuns, they cannot be soldiers, and they will not pay the taxes that support the military.

In our country we continue to spend countless millions of dollars on weapons systems. The tiny amount donated to peace projects over the years is probably equivalent to what is spent on one square inch of a nuclear submarine or on the trigger device of a single missile. The priorities of our society are plain, and even in a post-Soviet world we are far from being able to turn them around. Creating a new set of priorities will undoubtedly require a major effort. It calls for an effective strategy and a certain kind of passion or militancy. Obviously it must be a nonviolent militancy, one that is opposite in effect to, and more powerful than, the violent militancy that presently prevails.

In the course of history, when people have sincerely looked into their own minds, they have found a great deal of aggression there. Men in the past may have found a warrior armed with a spear, perhaps a Magadhan warrior about to slay a Kaliṅgan, as King Aśoka did. Those looking now might discover a gun or a bomb in their minds. If we are activists and find ourselves conducting protests full of hostility toward the bombmakers, the bombdroppers, the oppressors—all these supposed external villains—it means that we are harboring all sorts of villains in ourselves. Some of the people who have looked inward and found violence in their own minds realized they needed support to conquer it. They sought institutions that would allow them to devote their lives to self-conquest, a process that can only be accomplished nonviolently, from the inside, from the heart. It means working with psychological tendencies that have been established from beginningless time and have become nearly instinctive. To transform these patterns, a complete reconditioning program is necessary. Buddhist monasticism endured and flourished because it was designed to accommodate such a program.

Whether or not a society accepts monasticism is a revealing litmus test of that society. A community that supports institutions with a transcendent focus is genuinely dedicated to the liberation of its inhabitants. But if a society does not assent to monasticism, then everything is evaluated in terms of utilitarian purposes defined by the collective interest. Education becomes a tool for making citizens compliant and productive, while people who devote themselves to spiritual paths are considered nonproductive and worthless. A society that does not have a sanctuary for individuals striving wholeheartedly for release from birth-and-death is a society that does not value liberty in its deepest sense.

Shakyamuni's original strategy for conquering violence through nonviolence was intended to operate not only on an individual level but also on the scale of an entire society. If we reconsider the history of Buddhism from this perspective, we see that the creation of a monastic order was a precisely planned nonviolent movement. Tibet, perhaps more than any other nation, sought unreservedly to enact Shakyamuni's noble vision. It placed the monastic institution at the core of society, nurtured it devotedly, and aspired to actualize Dharmic values throughout the culture. We must not forget how effective this nonviolent strategy has been for many centuries, though obviously the work is by no means over.

The Dalai Lama's Prayer for Human Rights

Shakya Gelong Tenzin Gyatso, His Holiness the Dalai Lama, is the fourteenth representative of a lineage that has been a powerful force in Tibetan life since the fifteenth century. A Dalai Lama embodies a number of notable aspects. First, he is a Buddhist monk, a venerable member of the monastic army of peace that has just been described. When the present Dalai Lama was awarded the Nobel Peace Prize in 1989, he characteristically responded: "I am a simple Buddhist monk, no more, no less." Because Dalai Lamas have ruled Tibet since the seventeenth century, their human aspect also embraces the role of king. Beyond this level, a Dalai Lama is considered to be an incarnation of Avalokiteśvara, the bodhisattva of compassion. He is particularly associated with the thousand-armed form of Avalokiteśvara, introduced above, who took a vow to work on behalf of the Tibetan nation. A further dimension of a Dalai Lama derives from Vajrayana Buddhism. On this level, as we have also noted, a Dalai Lama is considered to be an emanation of the Kālachakra Buddha, responsible for maintaining the purified sphere in which all beings are evolving toward perfection. These human and divine aspects, which represent the major streams of the Buddhist tradition, fuse together in the person of the Dalai Lama.[7]

In 1959, after the massacre of Lhasa, the fourteenth Dalai Lama and his party fled to India. At that time of crisis and desperation, one of the Dalai Lama's first acts was to compose and promulgate a poem. It was set to music and has become profoundly significant for the Tibetan people, a nation-in-exile's anthem. In English it is sometimes called the Prayer for Human Rights. A more literal translation of the Tibetan title, *Dentsik Mönlam*, is "A Prayer of Words of Truth." This poem is a contemporary expression of the Buddhist tradition of nonviolence.

1
O buddhas of the past, present, and future,
O bodhisattvas, masters, and disciples,
Who command the glory of the boundless ocean of virtue,
Who care for suffering beings as a mother cares for her only child,
Please hear my anguished words of truth.

2
May you ever magnify the ten virtuous practices
Of the wise, adept upholders of the Buddha's Teaching.
These practices dispel the pains of both existence and extinction
And spread the glory of help and joy throughout the world.

3
Wretched beings are ceaselessly tormented by their sufferings,
Driven by the dreadful force of their evil karmic acts—
Please save them from unbearable terrors, sicknesses, wars, and
    famines,
And refresh their spirits in your ocean of bliss and joy.

4
Please look at the religious people of the Land of Snows,
Ruthlessly conquered by the cruel tactics of evil invaders,
And let the might of your compassion swiftly arise
To stop the terrible flow of their blood and tears.

5
The violent oppressors are also worthy of compassion.
Crazed by demonic emotions, they do vicious deeds
That bring total defeat to themselves as well as to others.
Please grant them the insight into right and wrong,
And bring them to know the glory of loving friendship.

6

Swiftly grant us the fortune to enjoy
The millennium of the union of secular and sacred,
And may the whole of Tibet spontaneously achieve
Our cherished hearts' desire of liberty.

7

May Avalokiteśvara, guardian of the Potala,
Graciously protect this people who have suffered many trials,
Have given up precious body, life, and all possessions,
For the Teaching and the nation that upholds it.

8

Finally, I pray there soon may come the brilliant dawn
Of the fruition of all the great vows to cultivate Tibet
That Avalokiteśvara, the protector bodhisattva,
Swore before all buddhas and celestial bodhisattvas.

9

By the force of interdependence, by the truth of ultimate emptiness,
By the compassion of the Three Jewels, by the words of truth,
And by the power of the law of causation,
May this prayer quickly and irresistibly be realized![8]

According to an ancient Indian notion, if one speaks the truth and sticks to it, one creates enough power to make the Ganges River flow backward. The basic teaching in this prayer is that the power of truth is far greater than any oppressor's military might. When the Dalai Lama wrote these verses, he had just been mobbed by Chinese soldiers, he was sick with a raging fever, and his countrymen were dying all around him. Even so, he wanted to make his people clearly realize that the power of prayer and compassion will ultimately liberate them. The poem reflects the Buddhist tenet that the "conquest" of peoples' hearts by the truth (*Dharma vijaya*) can only be accomplished nonviolently, through the free understanding of individuals.

The Dalai Lama opens the prayer by calling upon the buddhas of the past, present, and future, the bodhisattvas, and the great Buddhist saints. This supplication—and the entire poem—express the piety that has been so important throughout the history of Buddhism but is as yet undeveloped in the Buddhism of the West. As discussed earlier, the world of the Mahayana Buddhist is filled with beneficent beings who exist in ways that do not fit into conventional categories of material existence. These are called upon by believers who may or may not think of themselves as seekers after enlightenment, but who feel they need help in dealing with the darkness and difficulties they face. Buddhas and bodhisattvas are said to respond very kindly to sincere appeals of this nature.

In the second verse the Dalai Lama extols the "ten virtuous practices" of the monastic code: not killing; not stealing; not committing sexual misconduct; not lying; not using abusive speech; not slandering; not engaging in frivolous speech; not having a malicious mind; not having a greedy mind; and not holding false views about the nature of reality. While lay Buddhist practitioners also strive to uphold these virtuous practices, the Dalai Lama's praise for the "adept upholders of the Buddha's Teaching" here refers primarily to the monastic Sangha, the Buddhist army of peace. The Buddhist monastic way of life that has been carried down through history in various Asian countries contains a great deal of knowledge concerning the ways that minds and societies work. Without it, we cannot expect to have a Buddhism that stands up to the militarism of the age in which we live.

In the fifth verse the Dalai Lama truly manifests the attitude of a bodhisattva, whose nonviolence is natural and spontaneous. He prays for the Chinese, because "violent oppressors are also worthy of compassion." It is unthinkable for a bodhisattva to blame his misfortunes on another person or any external cause. We noted above that the Dalai Lama even appreciates how much the Tibetans have learned at the hands of their oppressors. Bodhisattvas typically take delight in making whatever sacrifices they can for the sake of other beings. As Luis Gómez and Christopher Chapple elucidate in their essays, many *Jātaka* tales tell how the Buddha in previous incarnations gave up his own life to help others.

The reference to the "millennium" in the sixth verse reflects the Tibetans' abiding faith in the long-term historical evolution of the planet. In the seventh and eighth verses the Dalai Lama, even though he is himself Avalokiteśvara, identifies with his human aspect and calls on the celestial bodhisattva to fulfill his ancient vow to protect Tibet. Having just escaped from Lhasa, where a hundred thousand of his people had been massacred, the Dalai Lama is saying, "Please stop their blood and tears, please stop this holocaust."

The final verse of the prayer invokes the powers of truth and compassion that will eventually triumph over physical force, military might, and the like. We err if we imagine that violence or evil can ever match the force of compassion. This power of the Buddha and the Dharma is so great that we are not entitled to bemoan the apparent deficiencies in our situation, whatever they may be. Western Buddhists sometimes complain that they will never be able to attain enlightenment because they do not have enough time to meditate, or because they live too far from a Buddhist center, or because their teacher did something wrong. Such attitudes betray a serious misunderstanding. According to time-honored Buddhist teachings, the existence of a buddha in our age (Shakyamuni) means that the external conditions for liberation are complete. From this perspective, the planet is perfectly arranged to facilitate our spiritual development. That is surely one of the messages that the Tibetans, amidst their stark adversity, have so eloquently conveyed to us.

Notes

1. Geshé Wangyal, *The Door of Liberation* (New York: Maurice Girodias Associates, 1973), 61.
2. Mark Tatz, trans., *Asaṅga's Chapter on Ethics with the Commentary of Tsong-Kha-Pa, The Basic Path to Awakening, the Complete Bodhisattva*, by Bodhisattva Yogacarabhumi (Lewiston/Queenston: Edwin Mellen Press, 1986), 70–72.
3. On the Chinese occupation of Tibet, see John F. Avedon, *In Exile from the Land of Snows* (New York: Alfred A. Knopf, 1984).
4. Edwin Bernbaum, *The Way to Shambhala* (Los Angeles: J. P. Tarcher, 1989), 79–105, 157–80.
5. P. L. Vaidya, ed., *The Mahāyāna Sūtra Saṅgraha*, Part I, in Buddhist Sanskrit Texts 17 (Darbhanga, India: Mithila Institute, 1961); Robert A. F. Thurman, trans., *Kāraṇḍauyūha Sūtra* (unpublished manuscript, 1980), 10–14.
6. Adapted from Robert A. F. Thurman, trans., *The Holy Teaching of Vimalakīrti* (University Park: Pennsylvania State University Press, 1976), 18–19.
7. See Dalai Lama XIV, *Freedom in Exile: The Autobiography of the Dalai Lama* (New York: HarperCollins, 1990). See also Roger Hicks and Ngakpa Chogyam, *Great Ocean: The Dalai Lama* (New York: Penguin Books, 1990).
8. His Holiness the Dalai Lama, *A Prayer of Words of Truth* (Dharamsala, India: Library of Tibetan Works and Archives, 1975), 1–6. This English version, based upon the original Tibetan, is indebted to an earlier translation by Sherpa Tulku and Khamlung Tulku. Reprinted by permission.

6

The Impact of Christianity on Buddhist Nonviolence in the West

by Cynthia Eller

Recent interest in Buddhist nonviolence and social action is intimately related to Buddhism's encounter with the West. There is of course a long-standing tradition of nonviolence in Buddhism, one that goes back to Shakyamuni himself, and it continues to be a source of practice and discussion in dominantly Buddhist cultures. However, Buddhism in the West is in constant interaction with the Judeo-Christian tradition—if only because most of its practitioners were raised in homes and/or a culture dominated by these religions. Although a number of religious and secular traditions have affected Western Buddhist approaches to nonviolence, this discussion will focus primarily on Christianity. When the search for a genuinely Buddhist nonviolence is filtered through the latent demands of a predominantly Christian conscience, what emerges is a new Buddhism and a new Buddhist ethics, no less valid than the many new Buddhisms that have been produced in the 2,500 years of the Dharma's movement eastward around the globe.

The problem Western Buddhists face in constructing a Buddhist non-violence is one of reconciling two different understandings of the relationship between self, other, and society—one Buddhist, the other Western and predominantly Christian. Both traditions experience a tension between self and world, and efforts to conceptualize and resolve this tension are integral to the shaping of their moral ideals, including the ideal of nonviolence. Whereas Buddhism sees this tension collapsing in the face of a deeper truth about the ultimate indivisibility of self and world, Christianity attempts to ease the tension while preserving the distinction. Buddhist social ethics keep the focus on the self and demand personal transformation (with the understanding that social transformation will follow naturally in its wake). Christian social ethics generally seek to harness the self in service to the other, in an explicit quest for social transformation that reflects the kingdom of God. In spite of this difference in their fundamental ethical orientations—their metaethics—we find that much of the substance of Buddhist and Christian ethics is similar, especially in regard to the practice of pacifism.

Buddhist Metaethics and Nonviolence

A natural place to begin a study of Buddhist nonviolence is with the precepts, for it is here that *ahimsā* (nonharming or nonviolence) occupies a leading role. Of the various lists of moral precepts proffered for layperson or monk across many schools of Buddhism, the great majority begin with the pledge to abstain from taking life. Like the sixth commandment of Moses—that one must not commit murder—the Buddhist precept to cherish all life is flexible of interpretation, but it has been the victim of less casuistry over the centuries than has the Judeo-Christian commandment not to kill. As one observer has stated, "The principle of non-killing is as near an absolute as one can get in practical Buddhist ethics."[1]

But how is this "near-absolute" of nonviolence justified in Buddhism? Why do Buddhists deem it important to follow this precept? Why, after all, should one bother to be moral? These are important questions in comparing Buddhist and Christian approaches to nonviolence, for the answers are not the same in the two traditions. The precept of nonviolence—and indeed the whole body of Buddhist moral practices (*śīla*)—is justified first on the grounds that it conduces to the attainment of nirvana for the practitioner. Some Western scholars of Buddhism have accordingly concluded that Buddhist ethics are egoistic, appealing only to the self-interest of the agent and his or her desire to attain enlightenment.

This point of view is not without support in Buddhist writings, where passages attributed to Shakyamuni claim that morality is nothing more than a useful tool in the quest for enlightenment. Ananda Gurugé asserts:

> The Buddha, in his characteristic manner, emphasized his attitude to moral teachings as only a means to an end rather than an end itself. Com-

paring the Dhamma to a raft, he ridiculed the man who out of gratitude carried on his shoulders the raft which helped him to cross the waters.[2]

From this perspective, Buddhist ethics are an instrumental good; their principal value is that they help one to achieve the ultimate good of nirvana. Nevertheless, morality is of great importance, for it is one of the most reliable techniques available for counteracting the evil dispositions (greed, hatred, ignorance) that bind individuals to illusion. Bhikkhu Silacara compares the moral precepts to a train "which carries all who will avail themselves of it to nirvana, or at least a certain stage of the distance . . . for there are no accidents, breakdowns on this railway."[3]

If morality is a means to the end of enlightenment, then immorality is damaging to the self, for it inhibits one's progress towards the goal. Morality is thus practical, and immorality foolish. As one Buddhist writer explains, "By allowing anger to arise, I am like someone who wants to hit another and picks up a burning ember or excrement and by so doing either burns or soils himself."[4] Furthermore, the consequences of immorality are far-reaching, for it not only affects one's present life but one's future lives as well: by killing or otherwise violating the precepts, one may be reborn in a lower realm of existence, unable to attain nirvana.

Are Buddhist ethics then solely directed toward serving the self, without attention to the needs, rights, or well-being of others? A number of commentators defend Buddhist ethics against this charge by asserting that the same moral requirements which assist one in achieving nirvana have another function, that of promoting a better existence between humans beings who have yet to attain enlightenment. Others concentrate their apologetics on the goal of nirvana itself, saying that it must not be misunderstood as narrowly selfish project: to uproot the causes of evil and suffering is to benefit others as well as the self. P. D. Premasiri speaks for the Theravadin school: "What is aimed at by such an ideal [the quest for nirvana] is not the production of a band of selfish seekers after individual salvation but spiritual leaders capable of setting the right moral pace for the whole society."[5] Robert Aitken draws a similar connection between the individual pursuit of enlightenment and the welfare of others, in Mahayanist terms:

> "Bodhisattva" is a compound Sanskrit word that means "enlightenment-being." There are three implications of the term: a being who is enlightened, a being who is on the path of enlightenment, and one who enlightens beings.[6]

Here the quest for nirvana is considered more effective in securing the welfare of others than the presumably more direct method of giving tangible aid, because so long as one is unenlightened one's efforts are bound to be clumsy and perhaps even counterproductive. As the Buddha reportedly taught, "It is not possible for one who is stuck in the mud to help out another; it is only possible for one who is not stuck in the mud to help out another who is stuck in the mud."[7]

But if Buddhist ethics are preliminary, a means to achieving the goal of nirvana, they are also secondary, the natural outgrowth of enlightenment. P. D. Premasiri explains:

> Once [liberation] is achieved, the Buddhist saint does not lapse into a state of inertia and inaction. Rather, by virtue of the new benevolence of heart that replaces the former selfishness, he is spontaneously moved to disinterested action for the well-being of humanity.[8]

Where the seeker follows the precepts out of self-interest, the saint acts spontaneously out of concern for the good of all. Without resort to moral rules or reasoning, the enlightened person is expected to react in a compassionate and skillful manner to his or her surroundings. In *The Mind of Clover*, Robert Aitken describes this enlightened morality:

> Clover does not think about responsibility, and neither did Shakyamuni [when he went to tell his friends of his enlightenment]. He simply arose from his seat and went looking for his friends. The clover simply puts down its roots, and puts up its leaves and flowers. Fundamentally, the no-thought of the clover and the no-thought of Shakyamuni are the same. They come forth, and their response to circumstances is to give nourishment.[9]

Clearly, Buddhist ethics include a concern for others, but this other-regardingness is only *implied*; it does not stand alone. Moral responsibility and compassionate action may be fruits of enlightenment, but they are not themselves the justification for seeking enlightenment. One can see why such an ethics would be puzzling to Westerners who identify morality by the one necessary and sufficient criterion of other-regardingness. To such eyes, Buddhist ethics are not ethics at all, but sheer egoism. Presumably if the quest for enlightenment harmed rather than helped others, it might be a pity, but the self's demand for this quest would still carry the day.

This interpretation, however, does great violence to the spirit of Buddhism, because it imposes a Western understanding of the relation of self and other on Buddhist ethics. The Buddhist doctrines of dependent co-arising and no-self establish a framework in which the advancement of the true needs of the self cannot possibly detract from the true needs of the other. In fact, the fundamental interests of self and other are so intimately tied together that one can conveniently concentrate on the true needs of the self as the best means for advancing those of the other. Ultimately, the self is an illusion, a construct of the mind that distracts one's attention from the far more important reality of the self's coexistence with the other in what some writers call "the large self." Seeking enlightenment is a process of stripping away this illusion of separateness and correctly perceiving reality, in which self and other do not compete because they are not differentiated.

This can be seen in the training of practitioners, who are directed toward a nondifferentiating identification with all beings through the cultivation of *mettā* or loving-kindness (the positive counterpart of *ahimsā*). The practitioner attempts to see the self not just in the other who sits in the same room or lives in the same monastery, but in the far-distant other who is nonetheless inseparable from the self. To be aware of the interconnectedness of all life is to experience the joys and pains of all living beings. As Sulak Sivaraksa writes in this volume, "We can only save ourselves when all humanity recognizes that every problem on earth is our own personal problem and our own personal responsibility." Robert Aitken gives a concrete example of this type of awareness:

> When I look at my camera, and in tiny print I read, "Made in Singapore," I reflect upon the women who are employed at the factory there for low wages, who have no room in their lives for anything creative. I reflect upon the American workers who have no jobs because the factory has moved to Asia. There is no quick remedy for this injustice, but awareness is the beginning of Right Action.[10]

The Vietnamese monk Thich Nhat Hanh provides a further illustration of the identification of self and other in this fragment from his poem "Please Call Me By My True Names":

> I am the child in Uganda, all skin and bones,
>   my legs as thin as bamboo sticks,
> and I am the arms merchant, selling deadly
>   weapons to Uganda.[11]

It is significant to note that the awareness expressed in these passages represents a change in perception, not a change in reality. Self and other do not need to be brought into a relation of interdependence, nor does the practitioner need to manipulate the needs of either self or other to make them more compatible. Thus the best one can do for others and for society is to cultivate one's self, and to act as consistently as possible out of a deep recognition of the interconnection of all living beings. To a mind nurtured on the separateness of self and other, this may seem to be a minute and ineffective contribution to solving the world's problems. But to the Buddhist mind, it is the largest and most effective contribution possible, for the thoughts and actions of the self do not remain encased in an isolated existence; they have consequences that can be felt at a great distance. As Thich Nhat Hanh explains: "Every action, every thought has an effect. Even if I just clap my hands, the effect is everywhere, even in faraway galaxies."[12] For Buddhist ethics, it might truly be said that the personal is political (to borrow a phrase from the feminist movement). Buddhist nonviolence begins in the mind and moves from there to affect the world without any additional or special effort on the part of the practitioner.

Christian Metaethics and Nonviolence

If Buddhist ethics resolve the tension between self and other by seeing them as ultimately coextensive, how does Christianity resolve this same tension? For Christians, self and other are not in conflict because of an error of perception; they are in conflict in actuality. And if this conflict is to cease, it is reality that must change, not just perception. Christian ethics, like Buddhist ethics, hope to transform the self so that it no longer experiences conflict with the other, but even when the transformation is complete, self and other remain as distinct entities with particularistic needs. However, the dream is that once the self is humbled and brought into proper relationship with God, it becomes possible for one to interact with others in mutual fulfillment of each other's needs. This ideal state is sometimes identified with the kingdom of God, a perfect society (either in heaven or on earth) where interpersonal conflict ceases under the benevolent rule of God or Christ.

The concept of the kingdom of God is far more prominent in Christian ethics than similar concepts are in Buddhism.[13] The kingdom of God is a complex doctrine, and it has been interpreted in a great variety of ways throughout Christian history. There is no real agreement among Christians as to what Jesus meant by the phrase "kingdom of God," but it is clear that it was inspired by both the Jewish belief in a God who acts in history and by Greek notions of the just and perfect ruler, such as one can find in Plato.[14] Benedict Viviano suggests that there are four major interpretations of the kingdom of God. The first two equate it with an earthly institution: the state or the church. Both of these interpretations have roots in early Christianity, but they flourished most noticeably under the Holy Roman Empire of the Middle Ages. The third interpretation views the kingdom of God as a future society which will come to earth at a time of God's choosing, while the fourth interpretation sees it as being either an inward experience or a next-worldly phenomenon.[15] Though these four approaches differ greatly on the question of what the kingdom is and how it already has or will come to be, the general theme is of a covenant between human beings and God which works to bring about an ideal society.

The goal here is social rather than individual: it is a society that is perfected through obedience and right relationship to God. Change is hoped for and anticipated on a communal level, with God (or God's agents) governing humankind. And in many versions of the kingdom of God ideal, Christians themselves—or the Christian church or state—are responsible for acting to make this kingdom a reality.

Where Buddhism begins with suffering and the search for its solution, Christianity begins with sin and the search for its redemption and forgiveness. It aspires to heal the breach between self and other so that an ideal (sinless) society can be constructed on earth or in heaven, and it accomplishes this by relaxing the claims of the self in deference to the claims of others. Christianity certainly advocates personal transformation, but it conceives the relationship between personal and social transformation differently than does Buddhism. Rather than beginning, as Buddhists do, by promoting the self's well-being in the conviction that the other's well-being will follow, Christian ethics begin by promoting the other's well-being in the conviction that this act of selflessness will, paradoxically, lead to the self's well-being (if not in this life, then certainly in the next). The difference is primarily one of emphasis, of picking up the fabric of individual and social life from different ends. For Buddhists, the other will be served if the self is transformed; for Christians, the self will be transformed if the other is served.

Thus when nonviolence is defended in Christian terms, it is strongly based on serving the other and acceding to the other's legitimate claims. Violence is forbidden not because it will cause harm to the self, but because it harms the other. This is particularly true when nonviolence is treated as a lifestyle and a spiritual commitment, as has generally been the case in traditional Christian pacifism. John Howard Yoder, for example, argues that Christian pacifism requires one to "abandon claims of justice for oneself and for one's own in an overriding concern for the reconciling of the adversary and the estranged."[16] However, when nonviolence is interpreted as a technique for achieving specific social ends, the self's legitimate claims move to the forefront of Christian nonviolence. It is because the self's claims are being ignored or overrun that one is able to justify a nonviolent campaign against the other. But in fact this assertion of self is strongly restrained. Rarely is it actually the *individual's* self-interest that is being promoted, but rather the interests of the group. It is as though the self's claims do not become legitimate or defendable until they are taken up by a community that shares them. Thus if the individual is being unjustly mistreated, Christian nonviolence would first recommend suffering silence with the assurance of God's pleasure. It is only when the well-being of others "like" one (in the same political or social condition) is at stake that one may marshal a campaign in which nonviolence is consciously used to bring about specific political ends. It is not the specific individual's pain that legitimates the nonviolent campaign, but the injustice and the violation of God's will committed by the other. The very determination to remain nonviolent in a political campaign is another concession to the claims of others (in this case, the right of the other not to be killed). Though the self's interests may be promoted at one level, there is always a point at which the nonviolent Christian must step back and acknowledge the claims of others in order to sanction the entire process as Christian.

Buddhist and Christian Pacifism

In spite of the differences in Buddhist and Christian understandings of the self/other distinction, and the resulting difference in moral foci, Buddhist and Christian pacifists have over the centuries demonstrated remarkable similarity in several respects. To begin with, they make similar arguments in favor of pacifism; although supported by differing metaethics, their stances are all but indistinguishable on the level of ordinary moral justification. Buddhist and Christian pacifists have also been situated similarly in a sociological sense, viewing themselves as partially or fully detached from politics, government, and the continued existence of the state. In addition, the means chosen by both groups to advance social progress have typically been oriented toward service rather than political action.

In defending their pacifism, both Buddhists and Christians regard voluntary suffering as an ideal form of moral action. The two *Jātaka* tales related in Luis Gómez's essay, the story of Speaker of Patience and that of the bodhisattva who offers himself as food for the tigress, dramatize this point. They valorize self-sacrifice and view it as a powerful way (a skillful means) of showing compassion for the suffering of others. In more recent times, the self-immolation of a number of Buddhists during the Vietnam War invoked this same theme. In a letter to a young Vietnamese woman named Chi Mai, who immolated herself in 1966 as a call for peace and reconciliation in Vietnam, her friend Cao Ngoc Phuong wrote:

> Your single sacrifice moved the hearts of countless others, Chi Mai, and made the peace movement swell like waves in a storm. Even friends who had joined the jungle guerrillas and had disappeared for a long time sent back news and asked, "How can we help realize Mai's wish and bring reconciliation?"[17]

Christianity likewise supports the idea of self-sacrifice, interpreting the crucifixion of Jesus as a demonstration of his compassion for suffering humanity. Modern Christian pacifists also laud the martyrdom of those who endure pain rather than inflict it, those who suffer in compassion for another's suffering.

Probably the most common arguments made by Buddhists and Christians in support of pacifism focus on "means and ends" and long-term consequences. According to both traditions, it is not possible to overcome evil with evil, or to use bad means to achieve good ends. P. D. Premasiri explains why:

> Buddhism's opposition to violence stems from the analysis that violence is psychologically rooted in *doṣa* (hatred). . . . Therefore, no matter what the intended merits of a projected social order may be, if it is established by violence it will have to be perpetuated through violence, for *doṣa* can only beget *doṣa*. Social change through nonviolent means is the only *realistic* path to a stable social order.[18]

The Christian pacifist position is reflected in Bayard Rustin's observation that the theory "that ends justify means, that from unfriendly acts a new and friendly world can emerge" is "a moral impossibility."[19] Common to both Buddhist and Christian pacifism is the conviction that because only good means will produce good ends, means and ends are not truly separable. As Robert Aitken concludes: "The practice of peace and harmony *is* peace and harmony, not some technique designed to induce them."[20]

A related notion that Buddhist and Christian pacifists embrace is the importance of long-term consequences. According to this line of reasoning, though evil means may appear to produce acceptable consequences in the short run, they always produce more misery and violence in the long run. A passage from the *Dhammapada* speaks for Buddhism: "Victory breeds hatred; the vanquished live in sorrow. The peaceful live in harmony, giving up both victory and defeat."[21] In 1970 Thich Thien-Minh similarly observed that "in Vietnam, violence has not worked for twenty-five years. Instead, violence has bred more violence."[22] When Christian pacifists are confronted with the possibility that violence may produce short-term benefits, they likewise appeal to the long-term victory of God's means, namely pacifism. In the words of John Howard Yoder: "The kind of faithfulness that is willing to accept evident defeat rather than complicity with evil is, by virtue of its conformity with what happens to God when he works among men, aligned with the ultimate triumph of the Lamb."[23] Yoder's faith in the long-term victory of God is paralleled in Buddhist pacifism by a faith in the power of the Dharma. Both traditions believe that love or compassion are ultimately stronger than evil, so eventual success is guaranteed (though success may be defined either as worldly transformation or as liberation from the constraints of the world). As Robert Thurman says in these pages, "We err if we imagine that violence or evil can ever match the force of compassion. This power of the Buddha and the Dharma is so great that we are not entitled to bemoan the apparent deficiencies in our situation, whatever they may be." Another important commonality between Buddhist and Christian pacifism is their view of the state. Both pacifist traditions assume a political disenfranchisement in the face of governments that they cannot control or aspire to control. For its first four centuries, Christianity was a minority movement and a pacifist one, with no access to state power. It did not renounce its pacifism until it gained control of the empire. Significantly, the pacifist sects which sprung up in later centuries were not formed by those with political power, but by those who lacked it. The state was regarded as a necessary evil, the kingdom of this world not to be confused with the kingdom of God. Political disenfranchisement has also been the lot of many Buddhists throughout history, and there is a similar reluctance among Buddhist pacifists to view the state as an appropriate agent for the advancement of human welfare. The great Buddhist philosopher Nāgārjuna, when asked by a king for advice, told the ruler that he should look first to his own enlightenment, even to the extent of neglecting the state. Robert Thurman says that "the practical impact of this advice is that the 'business of society' is just not that important."[24] Hajime Nakamura traces this sentiment back to the Buddha:

> Shakyamuni withdrew himself from the reign of kings as far as possible, and aimed at establishing an ideal society (Sangha) among recluses, thereby ameliorating society morally under the spiritual influence of Buddhism. He was not a politician who wanted to improve society with political power, nor a demagogue who used the passions of the populace for his own interests.[25]

The pacifism of the politically disenfranchised can be interpreted as "pacifism for lack of a better means." For those without access to political power, the only hope for personal and social efficacy is via some other mechanism, particularly one that avoids violence (which will most likely lead to the slaughter of the powerless). This reality helps to explain the somewhat peculiar element of self-protection in Buddhist and Christian nonviolence, the belief that by being nonviolent one is also warding off violence against oneself. Among the assumed advantages of pursuing *mettā*, the positive counterpart of *ahiṃsā*, is that "fire, poison, and weapons do not affect one."[26] Christian pacifists similarly expect a principled nonviolence to afford them some degree of protection, for if God's will is followed, one wins the power of God to one's cause.

The resort of necessity (or choice) to nonviolent means translates into a desire to view the personal as political. If the only avenue open to us is our personal and direct acts, and we hope nevertheless to have some effect upon the world, it is reassuring to believe that even though we are not acting on a world-historical stage, our actions still have an impact. As we have seen, Buddhist pacifism—and indeed Buddhist ethics in general—support this view. What is interesting is that Christian pacifism, though its guiding metaethics are quite different, also wants to claim that the seemingly small and limited acts of a politically disenfranchised individual are actually the best (only) means to usher in the kingdom of God. It is by tangible acts of mercy, the determination to be nonviolent, and the pledge to be faithful to God's will that the world is transformed.

Thus Buddhist and Christian pacifists, insofar as they are interested in transforming the world, generally favor direct service to others over political action. The Christian pacifist tradition has historically approached the task of social change by feeding the hungry, healing the sick, giving to the poor, etc. Buddhist pacifism has taken a similar tack when it has sought to be involved in society, by engaging in rural development, helping victims of natural disasters, building roads and canals, founding schools and nutrition programs, and so forth. American sanghas have become involved in similar forms of social service, such as "prison meditation projects, language instruction for immigrants, collections for disaster relief, efforts to rebuild inner-city community, work to end hunger and malnutrition, alternative health and child care, hospice support, refugee resettlement help, and more."[27] In all cases, the effort is small-scale, direct, and if not apolitical, at least not intent on seizing the reins of political or governmental power. Though there is a conviction that such service leads inexorably to increased social welfare, the immediate aim is to ameliorate suffering where it is found.

Buddhist Nonviolence in the West

Though there are significant commonalities between Buddhist and Christian pacifism, when Buddhism interacts with the West its first point of contact is not with the Christian pacifist tradition—a minority tradition at best—but with a more mainstream understanding of Christian ethics. The emphasis upon the claims of others, shared by Christian pacifists and non-pacifists alike, becomes in the hands of mainstream Christianity something quite different than the "personal-is-political" commitment to social service in Christian pacifism. Rather, what comes to the fore in mainstream Christianity is the notion of taking responsibility for the course of politics, of manipulating power blocs in an effort to ensure the well-being of all. As Buddhism is adopted by Christians, ex-Christians, Jews, ex-Jews,

and other Westerners, a tension surfaces between Buddhist understandings of social ethics (cultivate the self and society will follow) and the Christian desire to be involved in the forward motion of history. Western
Buddhists find themselves struggling for balance on the frequently shift-
ing turf of self, other, and society as these are understood in the two different traditions of Buddhism and Christianity.

This is the context in which the current discussion of Buddhist nonviolence in the English-speaking world takes place. Western proponents
of Buddhist nonviolence have no trouble identifying nonviolence within
the Buddhist tradition, but a "socially engaged" nonviolence—prompted
by Buddhism's encounter with the Christian demand for social relevance—is more difficult to uncover. The elements of a socially engaged
nonviolence are latent in the Buddhist tradition, but an overall concept of
social engagement is not at the forefront, and advocates of modern
Buddhist nonviolence are frank about admitting this. As Ken Jones la-
ments, "Buddhism has no explicit body of social and political theory comparable to its psychology or metaphysics."[28] Or as Nelson Foster comments, "It is remarkable that Zen lacks a clear tradition of social action.
One searches in vain for a body of teaching equivalent to the 'social gospel'
of Christianity."[29]

Some of these thinkers suggest that this "social gospel" or "social and
political theory" is precisely what the West (or Christianity) has to offer to
Buddhism. Through a melding of these two traditions, they believe, a
more complete philosophy of life and the world will come to light. Gary
Snyder takes this position when he says, "The mercy of the West has been
social revolution; the mercy of the East has been individual insight into the
basic self/void. We need both."[30]

For Western Buddhists, the tension between Buddhist and Christian
social ethics is most pronounced over the question of means. Though it is
not hard to persuade traditional Buddhists that the Christian vision of an
ideal society is indeed beneficial, it is far more difficult to reach agreement
about how one might appropriately and effectively realize this ideal. On
one side are those who advocate Buddhist nonviolence and social activism
as a tactic for accomplishing social ends, those who approve of such means
as "civil disobedience, outspoken criticism, protest, pacifism, voluntary
poverty, and even gentle violence if it comes to a matter of restraining
some impetuous crazy."[31] On the other side are more traditional Buddhists who believe that "our first work as peacemakers is to clear our minds
of mental conflicts caused by ignorance, anger, grasping, jealously, and
pride."[32]

Contemporary figures who see Buddhist nonviolence as a strategy
for accomplishing social ends are vague about exactly which means are acceptable, but they are clear in saying that the condition of the world calls

for a broadening of means beyond the simple effort to transform the self. Nelson Foster writes:

> For centuries, Zen people have habitually abstained from overt social action, preferring to let subtle good influence radiate from the temple gate into the body of society through a variety of means—a monk's model of selflessness, a teacher's influence on the ruler, the initiation of new cultural forms like the tea ceremony. Dr. Masao Abe aptly calls this "dissolving the root of social evil" and contrasts it to cutting back evil's branches through direct work for social or political change.
>
> We who share a devotion to this deepest, gentlest way of change may find it odious to admit that adhering strictly to it can block the reflex of compassion and leave us powerless to meet the problems of the present day. But admit it we must. Today it is not only natural to respond to the cries of the world; it is also necessary for our common survival. The human capacity to bring suffering and destruction upon ourselves and other beings has so broadened and accelerated that change through religious experience cannot alone suffice to save us. It is simply too slow. . . . We delude ourselves if we suppose that our zazen and its gentle good effects can alone have the corrective results that are now necessary for planetary survival.[33]

An opposing view is given by the Dalai Lama, who admits that cultivating the inner peace of the self may not provide a quick solution but insists that it is the only method which provides a certain solution. He writes, "The time has come to try a different approach. Of course, it is very difficult to achieve a worldwide movement of peace of mind, but it is the only alternative. If there were an easier and more practical method, that would be better, but there is none."[34]

This tension over means is also evident in discussions about how the individual Buddhist activist should monitor his or her involvement in social and political arenas. Chagdud Tulku advises, "As you meet the powerful, worldly men who sit at the top of the war machines, regard them with strict equanimity. Convince them as effectively as you know how, but be constantly aware of your own state of mind. If you begin to experience anger, retreat."[35] Christopher Titmuss also claims that there is a point at which practicing Buddhists must remove themselves from the world of politics, but he draws the line at a different place:

> There are of course some dangers in becoming socially engaged as a Buddhist. The main danger, as with all things, is the ego becoming increasingly involved in the act. . . . But wherever there are dangers, there are safeguards. . . . Firstly, self-observation. Once one gets so involved that one stops looking at oneself, I think it's time to forget political work.[36]

Titmuss's position seems more permissive, for presumably one could watch oneself becoming angry; but so long as one is monitoring this process, one need not give up action in the political sphere.

In fact, this monitoring of oneself in the midst of political activism is one of the two models of Buddhist nonviolence that have emerged in the West. Both of them are worth examining for their attempt (perhaps successful) to bring together Buddhist self-cultivation and a Western or Christian desire for nonviolent social action. This first model of Buddhist nonviolence can be called the "action meditation" model. Two of its defenses of political action were drawn from traditional Buddhist goals: the relief of suffering through service to others, and the construction of a society which supports the individual seeking enlightenment (the "social ethic" attributed to the Buddha). But several figures add a third defense of political action that is new: political activism as a way of pursuing enlightenment, as an exemplary forum for observing the habitual thoughts and behaviors of the narrow self.[37] According to the action meditation model, this kind of engaged self-cultivation is producing social transformation in the best tradition of Buddhist ethics. Not only is the meditator gradually freed from the narrow self by the practice of social activism, but the political community is also transformed through the presence of peaceful people. Advocates of this approach further suggest that the practice of meditation facilitates communication and cooperation among activists, thereby enriching and empowering the world of practical politics.

The action meditation model of Buddhist nonviolence is grounded in Buddhist thought, and it incorporates traditional Buddhist approaches to social ethics. Yet it also leaves room for a more pronounced activism by providing freedom to move on the political level. The price of this increased freedom may be a more relaxed attitude toward the acceptability of particular means. The advocates of this model have not yet formulated a consistent position on which means are permissible or optimal in the effort to gain social ends, nor have they taken a firm stance on which means are impermissible. One could imagine that fairly coercive means could become justified, if the situation seemed to warrant them and if Buddhist activists seemed able to coerce without being overwhelmed by the dispositions of greed, hatred, or ignorance. This potential cleavage between means and ends would not be in keeping with traditional Buddhist ethics; it would bear the stamp of mainstream Christianity's interest in purchasing social responsibility at the expense of ethical consistency.

A second and perhaps more satisfying model of Buddhist nonviolence might be called the "compassion-based" model. It has been promoted most prominently by the Vietnamese monk Thich Nhat Hanh, whose seminal teachings are discussed at greater length in Kenneth Kraft's essay. Nhat Hanh's version of Buddhist nonviolence resolutely refuses to separate means and ends, self and other. Yet it also remains open to more "activist" forms of nonviolence (such as political demonstrations), and it exhibits a more wholehearted devotion to the needs of others than one usually finds in traditional Buddhist pacifism. Where the action meditation model makes concessions to Western notions of political responsibility by making political action a Buddhist exercise in self-awareness, Nhat Hanh's Buddhist nonviolence relies on Buddhist metaethics to develop an other-regardingness that can potentially satisfy the crypto-Christian conscience.

In 1964 Nhat Hanh founded the Tiep Hien Order of Buddhism, a group that was very active for peace during the Vietnam War. Members of the Order demonstrated against the war, distributed written materials, initiated social service projects, supported draft resisters, and cared for the sick and injured. For Nhat Hanh, this involvement in political action was not merely an accident of the times, for he has said more recently that those who try to observe the precept of not killing "have to be working for peace in order to have peace in themselves."[38] Here and elsewhere Nhat Hanh engages in a reversal of the more traditional Buddhist formulation that those working for peace in themselves inevitably produce peace for the world. Yet Nhat Hanh does not embrace political activism to the exclusion of self-cultivation; instead he continually forges links between the two:

> Sometimes if we don't do anything, we help more than if we do a lot. We call that non-action. It is like the calm person on a small boat in a storm. That person does not have to do much, just to be himself, and the situation can change. That is also an aspect of Dharmakaya: not talking, not teaching, just being.[39]

Nhat Hanh is unwilling to compromise his principled commitment to nonviolence. He states, "If you think that violence is sometimes needed, then I think you need more awareness and more love. Then I am sure you will go in the other direction."[40] In a similar spirit, he persistently argues against the notion that there are "others" who must be defeated if the world is to have peace: "'Where is our enemy?' I ask myself this all the time."[41] The motivation that sustains peacework is compassion for others, a Buddhist concept with an obvious appeal for Christians. Yet instead of placing his emphasis on the Buddhist conviction that the best way to serve the other is to serve the self, Nhat Hanh refuses to make the separation between self and other, even for the sake of argument. As he explains:

> The kind of suffering that you carry in your heart, that is society itself. You bring that with you, you bring society with you. You bring all of us

with you. When you meditate, it is not just for yourself, you do it for the whole society. You seek solutions to your problems not only for yourself, but for all of us.[42]

This model of nonviolence places restrictions on appropriate means by requiring consistency between means and ends, but it is not rule-bound. Thus it appeals to mainstream Christianity's desire to answer the claims of others in a spontaneous, flexible, and personal manner. Thich Thien-Minh, a colleague of Nhat Hanh, relates the question of means to the spirit of Buddhist nonviolence:

> The techniques of nonviolent action are not nonviolent action itself. They are merely forms of action, not the essence. The essence is love, courage, and the willingness to act. Once we are motivated by love, once we are inspired by love, and when we directly face our problems and difficulties, we shall be creative in our efforts to find forms of action appropriate to a given situation. It is necessary to discuss techniques of nonviolent action, but it is equally obvious that, without the inspiration of love and sacrifice, these techniques cannot be successful. They will lack their deeper strength.[43]

Nhat Hanh's compassion-based model of Buddhist nonviolence remains faithful to Buddhist metaethics while achieving a tone that can resonate in Western ears sensitized to claims of other-regardingness and social activism. Robert Aitken reflects on the failures of the peace movement and his fear that it may not be possible to bring an end to war, saying, "The point is that, with all our good intentions, we are still seeking to advance and control the myriad things."[44] Though it requires a deep conviction that self and other exist in the web of dependent co-origination, Nhat Hanh's Buddhist nonviolence offers a way to step back from the desire to advance and control, without abandoning work for justice and peace, and perhaps most importantly, without abandoning hope.

Notes

The author wishes to express her gratitude to Kenneth Kraft, Serene Jones, Tom Bowman, Barry Seltser, Winston King, and Richard Kollmar for helpful readings of earlier drafts of this essay.

1. Winston L. King, *In Hope of Nibbana: An Essay on Theravada Buddhist Ethics* (LaSalle, Ill.: Open Court Publishing, 1964), 277.
2. Ananda P. Gurugé, "Some Problems in Buddhist Ethics," in J. Tilakasiri, ed., *Añjali: Papers on Indology and Buddhism* (Preadeniya: University of Ceylon, 1970), 5.

3. Bhikku Silacara, "Taking the Precepts," in Paul Dahlke, et al., "The Five Precepts," *The Wheel* 55 (1975), 10.

4. Hammalawa Saddhatissa, *Buddhist Ethics: The Path to Nirvana* (London: Wisdom Publications, 1987), 82.

5. P. D. Premasiri, "Ethics of the Theravada Buddhist Tradition," in S. Cromwell Crawford, ed., *World Religions and Global Ethics* (New York: Paragon House, 1989), 46–47.

6. Robert Aitken, *The Mind of Clover: Essays in Zen Buddhist Ethics* (San Francisco: North Point Press, 1984), 9.

7. K. N. Jayatilleke, "Ethics in Buddhist Perspective," *The Wheel* 175/176 (1972), 49.

8. Premasiri, "Ethics of the Theravada Buddhist Tradition," 47.

9. Aitken, *The Mind of Clover*, 137.

10. Ibid., 25.

11. Thich Nhat Hanh, *Being Peace* (Berkeley: Parallax Press, 1987), 63.

12. Ibid., 56.

13. Rough Buddhist counterparts to the Christian ideal of the kingdom of God can be found in a number of places. A picture of the ideal just society under the rule of the *cakkavatti* or ideal monarch can be found in early Buddhist texts: see Shanti Bhikshu Shastri, "Buddhist Ethics and Social Ideas," in L. M. Joshi, et al., *Buddhism* (Patiala: Punjabi University, 1969), 46; Hajime Nakamura, "Violence and Nonviolence in Buddhism," in Philip P. Weiner and John Fisher, eds., *Violence and Aggression in the History of Ideas* (New Brunswick: Rutgers University Press, 1974), 177–78; K. N. Jayatilleke, "Buddhism and Peace," *The Wheel* 41 (1969), 28. The Tibetan golden age of Shambhala is mentioned in this volume in Robert Thurman's essay "Tibet and the Monastic Army of Peace." During the Kamakura period in Japan, Nichiren reinterpreted the Pure Land not as a heavenly place of rebirth, but as a social order to be instituted on earth; see Daniel A. Metraux, "The Soka Gakkai's Search for the Realization of the World of Risshō Ankokuron," in *Japanese Journal of Religious Studies* 13:1 (1986), 57. Takeuchi Yoshinori also alludes to the Pure Land as an earthly eschaton in "Buddhist Peace of Heart," in Alistair Kee and Eugene T. Long, eds., *Being and Truth: Essays in Honour of John Macquarrie* (London: SCM Press, 1986), 274–75.

14. No doubt some of the difference between Buddhist and Christian metaethics can be attributed to their precursors. While Christianity developed in a Jewish and Greek context, where God was presumed to act in a history that moved ever forward (and, one could hope, upward) in a linear progression, Buddhism grew out of a Hindu context, where history (and in fact, the entire universe) moved in endless cycles. For Christianity, then, the perfect society is not only desirable but

possible. For Buddhism, society is less likely to improve dramatically, and thus liberation must initially be achieved on an individual basis.
15. Benedict T. Viviano, *The Kingdom of God in History* (Wilmington: Michael Glazier, 1988), 30–56.
16. John Howard Yoder, *The Politics of Jesus* (Grand Rapids: Eerdmans Publishing, 1972), 243.
17. Cao Ngoc Phuong, "Days and Months," in Fred Eppsteiner, ed., *The Path of Compassion: Writings on Socially Engaged Buddhism* (Berkeley: Parallax Press, 1988), 163.
18. P. D. Premasiri, "Ethics of the Theravada Buddhist Tradition," 62.
19. Bayard Rustin, letter to draft board, 16 November 1943, CPS Personal Papers, Document Group 56, Swarthmore College Peace Collection, Swarthmore, Pennsylvania.
20. Aitken, *The Mind of Clover*, 22–23.
21. *Dhammapada* 201, quoted in K. Anuruddha Thera, "Religion and Peace," *Dialogue* (Colombo), New Series 11:1–3 (1984), 5.
22. Thich Thien-Minh, "Non-Violent Action from a Vietnamese Buddhist Viewpoint," in Homer A. Jack, ed., *Religion for Peace: Proceedings of the Kyoto Conference on Religion and Peace* (New Delhi: Gandhi Peace Foundation, 1973), 132.
23. Yoder, *The Politics of Jesus*, 245.
24. Robert A. F. Thurman, "Nagarjuna's Guidelines for Buddhist Social Activism," in Eppsteiner, *The Path of Compassion*, 122.
25. Nakamura, "Violence and Nonviolence in Buddhism," 174.
26. Saddhatissa, *Buddhist Ethics*, 83.
27. Nelson Foster, "To Enter the Marketplace," in Eppsteiner, *The Path of Compassion*, 52.
28. Ken Jones, "Buddhism and Social Action: An Exploration," in Eppsteiner, *The Path of Compassion*, 73.
29. Foster, "To Enter the Marketplace," 48.
30. Gary Snyder, "Buddhism and the Possibilities of a Planetary Culture," in Eppsteiner, *The Path of Compassion*, 84.
31. Ibid., 84.
32. Chagdud Tulku, "The Power of Peace," in Eppsteiner, *The Path of Compassion*, 93.
33. Foster, "To Enter the Marketplace," 58–60.
34. Tenzin Gyatso (The XIVth Dalai Lama), "Hope for the Future," in Eppsteiner, *The Path of Compassion*, 7.
35. Chagdud Tulku, "The Power of Peace," 94.
36. Christopher Titmuss, "Interactivity: Sitting for Peace and Standing for Parliament," in Eppsteiner, *The Path of Compassion*, 188.
37. See, for example, Jones, "Buddhism and Social Action," 72; Titmuss,

"Interactivity," 185; and Charlene Spretnak, "Dhamma at the Precinct Level," in Eppsteiner, *The Path of Compassion*, 188.

38. Nhat Hanh, *Being Peace*, 98.
39. Ibid., 25.
40. Thich Nhat Hanh, "Please Call Me By My True Names," in Eppsteiner, *The Path of Compassion*, 38.
41. Ibid., 33.
42. Nhat Hanh, *Being Peace*, 47.
43. Thien-Minh, "Non-Violent Action from a Vietnamese Buddhist Viewpoint," 133.
44. Robert Aitken, "Gandhi, Dogen, and Deep Ecology," in Eppsteiner, *The Path of Compassion*, 89.

7

Nonviolent Struggle: An Effective Alternative

by Gene Sharp

Buddhists, along with everyone else, live in societies and political systems that influence people positively or negatively. It is therefore important even for those pursuing individual spiritual paths to give attention to these systems and the conditions they create. More specifically, can the Buddhist principle of nonviolence be practically applied in the real political world, or must it be compromised in acute situations? Our ability to think independently about this matter is most likely to increase once we distance ourselves somewhat from our previous views and from the standard answers offered by religious or political traditions. The following ideas are not presented to obtain immediate agreement, but rather to stimulate fresh thinking, so that each person can draw his or her own conclusions.

Buddhists and Political Violence

We cannot proceed to discuss the societal relevance of nonviolent principles, particularly those related to Buddhism, without first observing that the political conditions in predominantly Buddhist countries are not exemplary or notably nonviolent. Nor have the past ways of dealing with

politics, power, and national defense in Buddhist countries been adequate
either in ethical or practical terms. It is true that Buddhists have generally
avoided military crusades in the name of religion, and we see that the
countries which have threatened the world with nuclear destruction are
not Buddhist, but Christian and Communist. However, countries that are
predominantly Buddhist have experienced many kinds of internal oppression, and they have often been the victims of hostile outside forces. In
the nineteenth and twentieth centuries these external forces have included European colonialism, Japanese aggression, intervention by the
United States, and the activities of indigenous Communist parties whose
ideology originated in Europe.

If we review political conditions in the predominantly or formerly
Buddhist countries—Sri Lanka, Thailand, Cambodia, Burma, Laos, Vietnam, China, Tibet, and Korea—we see a series of international and domestic crises and disasters. Military dictatorships, Communist dictatorships,
coups d'état, foreign invasions and occupations, mass slaughter of civilians, and other forms of internal oppression have generated untold suffering in recent years. These situations cannot all be attributed to the consequences of European intervention. While visiting Thailand in 1984,
I was reminded that in the eighteenth century Buddhist Burma invaded
Buddhist Thailand, sacked the capital of Ayutthaya in 1769, and burned
the great library there, destroying precious historical records and Buddhist texts.

Many of the problems shared by these predominantly Buddhist states
relate to the use of violence in politics. Without violence, those international and domestic calamities could not have occurred. For example, the
same army which was organized to repel foreign aggressors may turn on
its own legitimate government, staging a coup d'état to establish a military
dictatorship. The same forces that engage in violence for national liberation can later slaughter segments of their own population presumed to be
politically unreliable, ideologically impure, or racially unacceptable.
These are among the practical risks of using violence in politics, aside
from the religious or ethical problems that arise.

Yet violence has frequently been an organized part of the political systems of Buddhist countries as well as European ones. This is because violence is perceived to be necessary in dealing with foreign aggression and
promoting other presumably good ends. In light of the Buddhist precepts,
especially *ahiṃsā* (noninjury or nonviolence to living beings), this assessment should be rather surprising to us. Buddhists seem to have encountered many of the same problems that Christians and devotees of other religions have faced. How can one live by one's principles in a very imperfect
world? How can one act effectively against tyrants and aggressors, while

holding to religious precepts that forbid violence and the killing of human beings?

It is commonly assumed that passive submission is the only alternative to the use of violence for worthy goals, such as repelling aggression. However, mere passivity may also be rejected as morally unacceptable and politically irresponsible. Presented with the option of violence or submission, many religious people have reluctantly accepted violence and rejected the full application of *ahiṃsā*. The perceived lack of alternatives accounts for the endurance of militarism. Though countless groups committed to peace have organized antimilitary protests, these sincere demonstrations have not caused whole societies to renounce violence. Nor have attempts to abolish war by seeking individual converts to pacifism been successful. Quite to the contrary, people have held on to military systems as tightly as ever, because they would not choose to be powerless in a threatening world. Even though people have long recognized that nuclear weapons could lead to widespread extermination rather than trustworthy defense, they have only recently been able to contemplate the possibility of meaningful reductions in nuclear arsenals.

In other words, those who have believed in ethical and religious systems that espouse nonviolence, but who have also sought to live in this world as it is and be responsible to their fellow human beings, have repeatedly found that they could not or would not abandon violence. Instead, they have usually chosen to violate their belief in nonviolence, hoping that the results of their own use of violence in resisting aggression or oppression would be preferable to passive submission to the violence of others.

This view is also encountered at times in the Buddhist tradition. Hajime Nakamura of Tokyo University has investigated the response of early Buddhism to the problem of invasions. He reports that there was an Indian Buddhist priest who went to China and was asked by the Chinese king, "When foreign armies are going to invade my country, what should I do? If we fight there will be many casualties. If we do not repulse them, my country will be imperiled. Oh, Master, tell me what to do!" Though the Buddhist priest was a pacifist, he had to take the problem of national defense seriously. He advised the king that because the king had a duty to protect his country, he must repulse the invading armies by military means. Nakamura concludes that wars were tolerated insofar as they were regarded as beneficial for the state and the people.[1]

Thus Buddhism joins many other religions and secular traditions in developing what might be called a "justified war" position: that under certain conditions, and with certain restrictions, government leaders must make use of military means. War is accepted as necessary to resist a greater evil and to achieve a higher good. However delicate the language that may be used, that position means killing human beings. Today in predominantly Buddhist countries, respect for life may be practiced by individuals, but taking life in civil or international wars is officially practiced by society as a whole. Governments in Buddhist countries act much the same as governments in Europe and elsewhere. This reality produces ethical and practical dilemmas for people who do not wish to develop their own spirituality in isolation from the problems of the world, desiring instead to influence the actual course of events in the direction of nonviolence.

Misconceptions about Nonviolent Resistance

The notion that violence is required as an alternative to submission because there is supposedly no other option is not a view based on ethical postulates. Rather, it is based on assumptions about political reality and the nature of society. The assertion that there is no viable alternative is an empirically testable proposition, which turns out to be inaccurate. People who have been forced to justify war on ethical grounds have often been working from an incomplete or erroneous understanding of society and politics. Yet violence is not the only way to wield power. Military action is not the only effective response available to combat tyranny, injustice, and foreign invasion. As the historical cases presented below will demonstrate, nonviolent action, or nonviolent struggle, is a realistic and potent alternative.

Many false notions about nonviolent action can now be discarded on the basis of greater knowledge. One is that charismatic leaders are required in a nonviolent campaign. Another misconception is that people must have certain ethical beliefs or religious experiences before they can use nonviolent methods. On the contrary, there is a constant history of ordinary human beings who inventively waged nonviolent struggle, even when it seemed impossible. Nonviolent action is as much a Western phenomenon as an Eastern one; indeed, it is probably more Western, if one takes into account the labor movement and the resistance of oppressed nationalities.

Nonviolent resistance was not invented by M. K. Gandhi. Although Gandhi was deeply influenced by religious texts, he also recognized the political applications of nonviolent options. He knew that during the Russian Revolution of 1905, a powerful general strike forced the reluctant Csar Nicholas to grant the formation of a nominal parliament. Of the general strike Gandhi said, "We, too, can resort to the Russian method against tyranny." Referring to the Chinese boycott of American goods around 1900 (a protest against anti-Chinese legislation in the United States), Gandhi declared, "We must admit that our people have learned these tactics from China." He was similarly aware of ecclesiastical disobedience in England, American colonial tax refusal, and the Bengali boycott movement against the British. In South Africa, certain tax laws and pass laws had been nonviolently opposed by Muslims, Hindus, and Africans; Gandhi cited their disobedience as evidence that Indians could also practice such resistance.[2]

We often hear that nonviolent resistance is quite impossible for human beings because of our animal nature or our human nature. Ethnologists and others have told us that human aggressiveness and violence are based in our animal nature—a conclusion that is of course a great insult to the animals! To the contrary, animals can be very skilled in the use of nonviolent resistance, as our pets often demonstrate. I once had a highly intelligent Dalmatian, whom I would order to "Lie down and stay!" She didn't want to do either, so she crouched down and crawled along the floor without raising her height. A Great Dane I adopted when she was two always wanted to ride in the front seat of my truck instead of the back. I would command and cajole, but she would just look straight ahead as though I did not exist. After yelling and venting anger without effect, in desperation I tried to lift her over the seatback into the rear of the truck. She then went limp!

You, too, have probably been very good at nonviolent resistance, especially when you were young (and expressing "human nature" spontaneously). Children can obey the letter of an order while totally disobeying its intent. Even as a small child, you realized that violence against a powerful parent was highly counterproductive, bringing down overwhelming repression that you could not handle. So, if you felt unjustly treated (and especially if you did not like the food that meal), you just refused to eat. That was the beginning of a "hunger strike." If you were supposed to take out the garbage, you would claim you had to study furiously. That was the seed of a "refuse workers' strike." When you were supposed to clean up your room, you postponed doing it for weeks. It was deliberate "stalling and procrastination." Finally, after threats of dire consequences, you rearranged the piles and stuffed some things under the bed—the start of a "disguised disobedience campaign." When you were about to be walloped by the frustrated authoritarian figure in your family, and the other parent was in a room nearby, you screamed like mad—although you hadn't been touched. The other parent would run into the room and demand, "What are you doing to that helpless child?" It was the "martyr syndrome"—using the appearance (or the reality) of innocent suffering to advance a cause. Outside the house, when you refused to buy candy any more from a certain store after the owner snapped at you one day, you initiated an "economic boycott."

For better or worse, such behavior is common to all of us. We need to recognize that fact and its implications. Among adults, this resistant behavior is often apparent in people who insist they do not believe in non-violence or in turning the other cheek. Indeed, they may simply desire to be stubborn or obnoxious, by not doing what they are supposed to do and instead doing what is prohibited. Conduct of this type, whatever its motives, shows that we are capable of resisting without violence, without injuring or killing. When this stubborn behavior is carried out by groups of individuals acting together, it leads to people marching down the streets, holding vigils, conducting economic boycotts, and so on. Basic human cussedness is also expressed in labor strikes, in which people have said, "We will not work until these conditions are changed."

Nonviolent Struggle in History

Nonviolent struggle has an extensive and varied history. The scholarly investigation of this history has focused principally on Western countries, so we do not yet have ample data from Buddhist cultures, but it is clear that the methods of nonviolent struggle are equally applicable in the East and the West. One of the most common classes of methods of nonviolent struggle is *nonviolent protest and persuasion,* through verbal and symbolic expressions of a position or a grievance. Letters, petitions, leaflets, teach-ins, lobbying, picketing, mock awards, vigils, marches, religious processions, demonstrative funerals, and silence are among the activities that have been effective in diverse situations.

In South Vietnam in 1963, Buddhist monks and nuns nonviolently protested against the anti-Buddhist policies of the pro-Catholic regime of Ngo Dinh Diem. They displayed religious flags in defiance of a government decree, presented petitions, sang satirical songs, and were arrested by the thousands. Buddhists also engaged in fasts and committed self-immolation (not a nonviolent method). In response to Diem's brutal raids on Buddhist pagodas, Foreign Minister Vu Van Mau resigned his post, and the United States withdrew its support from Diem's administration. The regime was fatally undermined by the nonviolent resistance, although the final blow was a military coup.[3]

Ordinary people have often improvised forms of nonviolent protest in exceedingly difficult situations, even in the face of genocide. We are now learning more about a large demonstration that took place in Berlin in February 1943, when a final roundup of Jews had been ordered. Jewish men married to non-Jewish women were placed in a special prison in the Rosenstrasse. Their wives and some other relatives learned where they were, gathered outside the prison, and demanded that the husbands be released. The protesters organized themselves and kept vigil there in shifts, day and night, only a short distance from Gestapo headquarters. Despite repeated threats that they would be shot, they continued their defiance. "A few salvoes from a machine gun could have wiped the women off the square, but the SS did not fire, not this time," wrote one of the survivors. Finally, after about nine days and nights, the Jewish prisoners were released. "And the public eye missed the flickering of a tiny torch which might have kindled the fire of general resistance to despotism," the survivor observed.[4] Some of the men who were saved and the women who demonstrated are still alive and have recently been interviewed. Without this research, that important piece of the history of resistance to Nazism would have disappeared, and many people would conclude that only by violence could Nazis or genocide ever be resisted.

Nonviolent resistance does not work simply by protest and persuasion. A second category of nonviolent methods, *noncooperation*, involves the deliberate defiance of certain existing relationships—social, economic, or political. People may boycott selected products, stop work, refuse to pay taxes, disobey laws they regard as immoral, or simply ignore their opponents. Such nonviolent actions effectively delay or halt normal operations. For example, how can the legal system operate if the lawyers do not appear, the judges do not enforce the laws, and the court officers walk out? Or how can the transport system run if the truckers, the railway workers, and the airline employees go on strike? Civil servants and bureaucrats can easily be obstructive even in the best of times! Acting patriotically on a massive scale, they can deny would-be oppressors the use of the governmental system.

In recent years in the United States we have seen consumer boycotts of lettuce, grapes, and coffee in response to perceived injustices at home and abroad. We also experienced the Arab oil embargo of 1973, a form of international economic noncooperation. Two centuries ago, noncooperation was used successfully by the English colonies in North America. From 1765 to 1775, the colonists built up their own institutions and bypassed British laws. Many of the English governors and officials soon recognized the power of these methods. During the Stamp Act resistance, Governor Colden of New York admitted that he had no power outside the fort he commanded. Governor Bernard of Massachusetts Bay explained to London officials why he could not carry out instructions to distribute the stamps: "At this time I have no real authority in this place." The Lieutenant Governor added, "In the capital towns of several of the colonies and of this in particular, the authority is in the populace; no law can be carried into execution against their mind."[5] When U.S. history textbooks fail to point out the nonviolent aspects of the early American struggle for independence, they overlook an important lesson of that period.

Noncooperation was even government policy in Germany in 1920, in response to a coup d'état that sought to oust the democratic Weimer Republic. When Wolfgang Kapp and his troops marched into Berlin on

March 12, the president fled but proclaimed that he still headed the legal government. In a spontaneous display of resistance to the Kappists, civil servants stayed home, laborers went on strike, and ordinary civilians talked with and taunted the paramilitary troops on the streets. Officials in the provinces refused to cooperate, bankers at the Reichsbank would not release money to the usurpers, and various specialists declined to become part of the authoritarian regime. The new government could not even get typists to prepare press releases for the newspapers because the secretaries all stayed home, having locked their typewriters in closets. Though demonstrators were shot and killed on the streets, the population repudiated the coup within a week, and the paramilitary troops withdrew from Berlin.[6]

During World War II, Norwegian teachers similarly defied their rulers in Nazi-occupied Norway, refusing to join a fascist teachers organization or to use their positions in the schools to indoctrinate children.[7] In 1944, this type of action disintegrated dictatorships in El Salvador and Guatemala, two ruthless regimes that had killed thousands of people. General Jorge Ubico, who had ruled Guatemala since 1931, found his power dissolving in the face of massive and nonviolent noncooperation. As one observer wrote:

> Energetic and cruel, Jorge Ubico could have put down an armed attack. . . . He could have imposed his will on any disgruntled group, military or civilian, and stood its members up against a wall. But he was helpless against civil acts of repudiation, to which he responded with violence, until these slowly pushed him into the dead-end street where all dictatorships ultimately arrive: kill everybody who is not with you or get out.[8]

Various forms of nonviolent struggle have been practiced in South Africa. Despite all the past rhetoric of violence and all the acts of violence, the main means of African resistance have been strikes, demonstrative funerals, civil disobedience, and economic boycotts. Since Nelson Mandela's release from prison in February 1990, the African National Congress has been conducting talks with the government, relying upon both international diplomacy and "mass [nonviolent] struggle" to further its cause. In its first three years (December 1987–December 1990), the Palestinian *Intifada* in the Israeli-occupied West Bank and Gaza also remained largely nonviolent. Massive noncooperation, tax boycotts, strikes, resignations of civil servants, and the establishment of independent Palestinian institutions have proven more effective than earlier PLO terrorist acts in advancing the Palestinians' cause.

Though largely unnoticed by the world press, the Buddhist monks of Burma (renamed Myanmar) in the fall of 1990 initiated a significant noncooperation campaign. For decades the oppressive Burmese military regime has indiscriminately imprisoned, tortured, and killed leaders of the opposition, students, and monks, as was hauntingly revealed by the mass shootings of nonviolent demonstrators in Rangoon in September 1988. Though a 1990 election gave victory to a democratic opposition party, the ruling regime flagrantly ignored the election results. In an apparently spontaneous gesture of defiance, monks throughout the country stopped conducting religious ceremonies for soldiers or their families. Burma is still a devoutly Buddhist country despite thirty years of dictatorial rule, so the monks' refusal to accept offerings from soldiers constituted a serious challenge to the military government's legitimacy. In late 1990 troops brazenly invaded monasteries, and conciliatory pledges were extracted from Buddhist elders, but the ultimate outcome of these developments is not yet known.

Nonviolent intervention, a final category, is a way to interfere in a situation—and disrupt it—by nonviolent means. Hunger strikes, sit-ins, pray-ins, nonviolent obstruction, overloading facilities, setting up alternative systems of communication, establishing a parallel government, and countless other techniques can properly be called "weapons" of nonviolent intervention. Here we are not discussing "unarmed resistance." On the contrary, nonviolent struggle is armed with an abundance of psychological, social, economic, and political ammunition.

In March 1971, twenty-four Jews in Moscow engaged in sit-ins at the Supreme Soviet, demonstrating for the right to emigrate. That month alone, more Jews were permitted to emigrate than the 999 permitted for the whole of 1970.[9] In the Philippines in the spring of 1986 we witnessed many forms of nonviolent struggle against the regime of President Ferdinand Marcos. Following the murder of Benigno Aquino, the people decided they would no longer put up with official deceit and repression. The opposition movement succeeded in discrediting a fraudulent election, religious leaders repudiated the Marcos regime as illegitimate, the masses demonstrated in the streets, and members of the armed forces refused to obey orders. Civilians nonviolently intervened in the situation by filling the streets to protect the mutinous soldiers, effectively blocking loyalist tanks. The establishment of a parallel administration further destabilized the existing government and prepared for a transfer of power. After the inauguration of Corazon Aquino, Marcos resigned under popular pressure and hastily boarded a jet to Hawaii.

In ten years of struggle, the Poles succeeded in liberating themselves using most of the principal means of nonviolent action. They knew that if they revolted violently, the (former) Soviet Union could have retaliated with overwhelming force. So they chose to resist by doing things that were forbidden and by refusing to do many of the things they were supposed to do. Even under martial law, the Solidarity movement remained active. On a daily basis the Polish people gave up familiar patterns and took great risks, advancing their cause through underground organization, symbolic actions, and sheer persistence. Hundreds of illegally published newspapers, magazines, and books were issued each year in Poland. The people established a de facto free press, just as they had earlier established freedom of religion through the resistance of the Roman Catholic Church and other groups.[10] In 1989 Solidarity won the prime minister's office as well as a majority of seats in the Sejm, and in 1990 Solidarity leader Lech Walesa was elected president of Poland.

Nonviolent struggle has also been improvised for purposes of national defense. In 1968 and 1969, Czechoslovakia was invaded by its own allies, including the Soviet Union. Although Soviet troops and officials were distributed throughout the country, they could not find enough Czech and Slovak collaborators to enforce their plans. Even the Communist Party became a resistance organization against the Russians, as the National Assembly continued to meet and issue denunciations of the invasion. Journalists, refusing to collaborate, instead produced resistance newspapers, and the Czech police distributed these papers throughout the capital by smuggling them in police cars. The transport workers on the railways surreptitiously shunted the trains around so that they passed the same stations more than once, causing delays and confusion. Special difficulties were encountered by a train carrying Russian tracking equipment intended to locate the radio transmitters informing citizens of the resistance.

In Prague, the Czech students surrounded Russian tanks and employed a very potent nonviolent strategy—the subversion of an invader's troops. Their courageous behavior is documented in some extraordinary pictures and films. The tank crews, who were supposedly putting down a counterrevolution, climbed out to see what was going on. Why were these students passing out leaflets, talking to them, challenging their presence? Many of the Russian officers and soldiers on the streets of Prague could not endure the psychological pressures of this reception. Sadly, there were even two or three cases of suicide. It became necessary for the Russians to rotate their troops out of Prague; troops from Asian peoples in the Soviet Union were prominent among the replacements, because the students could not talk with them in Russian about the invasion. Even though the Czechs had no training in nonviolent struggle, their resistance held off political control for at least eight months, something that prepared military defense could never have done.[11]

Years later, a Russian gentleman came to see me at my Harvard office. After considerable discussion, he finally asked what I thought of the events in Czechoslovakia. I turned the question back to him, saying that I had heard it was necessary to rotate troops out of Prague every four days because the psychological pressures made them unreliable. Was it true? He leaned forward and exclaimed, "Not only in Prague—throughout the whole country. It was necessary!" What kind of war is it when not even one soldier has been killed but you have lost your whole army in four days?

In late 1989 the power of nonviolent struggle was massively demonstrated in Eastern Europe. In a few short weeks the Communist dictatorships in East Germany, Czechoslovakia, Bulgaria, and (with significant violence) Rumania fell when confronted by people power. The failure of the Soviet hardliners' coup of August 1991 was yet another triumph for nonviolent resistance.

Implementing Nonviolent Alternatives

Nonviolent struggle exists, and therefore it can be used in the future. It is necessary to reiterate these points, because people still offer the most sophisticated analyses to the effect that nonviolent struggle is impossible: we have the wrong kind of economic system; our animal nature or human aggressiveness cannot be overcome; we have been warped by our education or family structure or toilet-training or whatever. All these supposedly persuasive objections are misplaced, because nonviolent struggle endures. As Kenneth Boulding says, "That which is, is possible."[12]

One issue that will continue to generate discussion among certain religious believers is the degree to which nonviolent struggle requires some kind of personal transformation. Several of the essays in this volume present the classic Buddhist tenet that one's inner mindstate and one's social behavior are inextricably linked. Other traditions similarly focus on the spiritual awareness of those who wish to participate in a nonviolent movement. At the least, a high degree of courage is demanded. Gandhi, who believed that "the use of nonviolence requires greater bravery than that of violence," declared that "cowardice and *ahimsā* do not go together any more than water and fire."[13]

Is it also necessary to "love" one's opponent? Some Buddhists, Christians, and others have argued that "nonviolence" properly flows from compassion, and that hatred or malice should therefore have no place in nonviolent action. In practice, it may not always be necessary to set such high standards. While it is true that the impact of the nonviolent technique is often enhanced when activists are able to refrain from hostility, that same technique has been successfully applied by people who hated their opponents and desired to coerce them. From a political standpoint, nonviolent struggle remains effective whether or not it is religiously motivated. Another option was articulated by the Mississippi journalist who said, "I always love my enemies because it makes them mad as hell."[14]

Even if we conclude that "human nature" need not or will not be changed, even if we concede that mass conversions to pacifism are not going to occur, such considerations should not deter us from the task at hand. It is time to take the historical cases of unrefined nonviolent struggle and study what makes them successful or unsuccessful. Then we need to learn how to apply them to situations that we now believe can be handled only by violence and war, situations in which morally sensitive people have felt they had to compromise their belief in nonviolence.

Generally speaking, a nonviolent campaign can achieve success in four ways. The first is by conversion—winning the hearts and minds of the opposing faction. For many religious groups, the opponents' conversion to the values and goals of the nonviolent movement is the only true victory. Others, however, will accept accommodation by the opponents as a second route to success. Even if conversion is not gained, the opponents may decide it is too costly or too threatening to continue to fight, and they will grant concessions, negotiate a settlement, or submit to third-party mediation. A third possibility is nonviolent coercion: in the face of massive and uncompromising resistance, the opponents may be forced to concede against their will. Finally, if the opponents' sources of power are nullified to a sufficient degree, their system or government may disintegrate. Thus, changing the adversary's way of thinking is only one of several ways to achieve success through nonviolent means.

Though participants in nonviolent movements sometimes get killed, this alternative results in far fewer casualties than guerrilla struggles or conventional wars, to say nothing of nuclear bombing. Casualties in nonviolent actions often serve to advance the cause of those who have died, by increasing the resistance of their compatriots and by undermining the authority of their opponents. The tragic massacre of the student protesters in Beijing in the spring of 1989, whatever its short-term effects, does not necessarily mean the end of the Chinese democratic movement or its use of nonviolent methods. We need only recall that in India the Amritsar massacre of 1919 turned Gandhi into a supporter of Indian independence, and in Russia the slaughter of peaceful marchers in St. Petersburg on Bloody Sunday triggered the Russian Revolution of 1905.

It is conceivable that whole societies can be trained to carry out this kind of resistance in defense crises. "Civilian-based defense" is a policy that utilizes nonviolent civilian action to protect society against internal usurpations and external invasions. Employing many of the methods that have just been surveyed, it would aim to make the populace unrulable by aggressors and to deny tyrants their objectives. If such a strategy became viable and was perceived accordingly, it could deter an initial attack.

Civilian-based defense would require a certain level of support for nonviolent options among the general population, including those who now believe in military means. The merits of such a policy must therefore be demonstrated through careful research and analysis. Many questions need to be addressed: How can nonviolent resistance meet the defense requirements of a particular country? To what degree will people have confidence in nonviolent struggle? How skillfully can it be applied? In what ways can individuals and groups prepare themselves to implement it? What are the wisest strategies to develop and use? Depending on the answers, a country might then begin to add a nonviolent resistance component, on a modest scale, to its overall defense policy. Switzerland and Sweden have already done so. Several other European countries have conducted small-scale governmental or military investigations of civilian-based defense.[15] In a post-Cold War world, civilian-based defense could provide a viable alternative to the pointless proliferation of technological weaponry.

Living by a principle of nonviolence is not simply a bilateral relationship between the individual and the principle. We must also take into account our social and political situation and the responsibility we feel toward our fellow human beings. When tensions exist between the apparent demands of the principle, the individual, the situation, and social responsibility, what is the appropriate course of action? For those who see that nonviolent struggle is a possible response to acute conflicts, the range of political and ethical choices is broadened significantly. People who believe in "not killing" but who still want to struggle for freedom and justice now have a satisfactory course of action. They may also take the lead in developing nonviolent solutions to other social problems besides war.

Exploring the history and the potential of nonviolent struggle, one begins to realize that the "ethical" and the "practical" are essentially congruent. The nonviolent behavior espoused by the great religious teachers is ultimately that which works politically. Buddhists have long realized that violence breeds more violence, war breeds more war. In this decade alone, how many tyrants have discovered that by resorting to violence they have only prepared the way for their own political demise? All that was left for them to decide was how they should leave the country.

As more and more societies learn of the efficacy of nonviolent forms of resistance, we will see less reliance upon war and a corresponding empowerment of populations. People aware of nonviolent action need no longer be passive in the face of tyranny. The tension between being politically responsible and ethically steadfast can be resolved through nonviolent struggle. Then the basic principles of the great religions, applied strategically to the world's pressing conflicts, will reveal themselves also as the basis of the highest pragmatism.

Notes

1. Hajime Nakamura, "Violence and Nonviolence in Buddhism," in Philip P. Weiner and John Fisher, eds., *Violence and Aggression in the History of Ideas* (New Brunswick: Rutgers University Press, 1974), 178.

2. M. K. Gandhi, *The Collected Works of Mahatma Gandhi*, vol. 5 (Delhi: Government of India, 1961), 44, 329, 418, and 462. See also Gene Sharp, *Gandhi as a Political Strategist, with Essays on Ethics and Politics* (Boston: Porter Sargent, 1979), 23–41.

3. Adam Roberts, "Buddhism and Politics in South Vietnam," in *The World Today* (London) 21:6 (June 1965), 240–50; "The Buddhists, the War, and the Vietcong," in *The World Today* 22:5 (May 1966), 214–22.

4. Heinz Ullstein, *Spielplatz meines Lebens* (Munich: Kindler Verlag, 1961), 338–40. Quoted in Gene Sharp, *The Politics of Nonviolent Action* (Boston: Porter Sargent, 1973), 89–90.

5. Walter H. Conser, Jr., Ronald M. McCarthy, David J. Toscano, and Gene Sharp, *Resistance, Politics, and the American Struggle for Independence* (Boulder: Lynne Reinner, 1986). See also Pauline Maier, *From Resistance to Revolution: Colonial Radicals and the Development of American Opposition to Britain, 1765–1776* (New York: Vintage, 1972).

6. Donald J. Goodspeed, *The Conspirators: A Study of the Coup d'État* (New York: Viking Press, 1962), 108–43, 211–13. See also S. William Halperin, *Germany Tried Democracy: A Political History of the Reich from 1918 to 1933* (Hamden, Conn.: Archon Books, 1963), 168–88.

7. Sverre Steen, ed., *Norges Krig 1940–1945*, vol. 3 (Oslo: Gyldendal Norsk Forlag, 1947–1950), 73–105.

8. Mario Rosenthal, *Guatemala: The Story of an Emergent Latin American Democracy* (New York: Twayne, 1962), 200–202. Quoted in Sharp, *The Politics of Nonviolent Action*, 93.

9. Leonard Schroeter, *The Last Exodus*, (New York: Universe Books, 1974), 178.

10. Neal Ascherson, *The Polish August: The Self-Limiting Revolution* (New York: Viking Press, 1982). See also Lawrence Weschler, *Solidarity: Poland in the Season of its Passion* (New York: Simon & Schuster, 1982).

11. Fred H. Eidlin, *The Logic of 'Nonalignment': The Soviet Intervention in Czechoslovakia of 21 August 1968 and the Czechoslovak Response* (New York: Columbia University Press, 1980). See also H. Gordon Skilling, *Czechoslovakia's Interrupted Revolution* (Princeton: Princeton University Press, 1976); and Robert Littell, ed., *The Czech Black Book* (New York: Frederick A. Praeger, 1969).

12. Quoted in Jerome D. Frank, *Sanity and Survival: Psychological Aspects of War and Peace* (New York: Random House, 1968), 270.

13. M. K. Gandhi, *Nonviolence in Peace and War*, vol. 1 (Ahmedabad: Navijivan, 1945), 131–32; Gopinath Dhawan, *The Political Philosophy of*

Mahatma Gandhi (Ahmedabad: Navijivan, 1962), 72. Quoted in Sharp, *The Politics of Nonviolent Action*, 456–57.

14. Sharp, *The Politics of Nonviolent Action*, 790.

15. Gene Sharp, *Making Europe Unconquerable: The Potential of Civilian-based Deterrence and Defense* (New York: Ballinger, 1986). See also Gene Sharp, *Civilian-Based Defense: A Post-Military Weapons System* (Princeton: Princeton University Press, 1990).

8

Buddhism and Contemporary International Trends

by Sulak Sivaraksa

The Buddhist approach to world peace demands self-awareness and social awareness in equal measure. Buddhism does not assume that if only
everyone professed Buddhist creeds, or meditated with Buddhist
methods, then the world would be a better place. Nor does Buddhism
claim that the source of all war and oppression is found in the mind. As the
essays in this volume have shown, a fundamental tenet of Buddhist doctrine is the co-arising of mind and matter. The world in which we live includes cultural, socioeconomic, and military structures as well as
psychological realities. It follows that karma is simultaneously individual
and social. Merely tinkering with one link in the complex circle of causation does not stop the process that leads to violence and warfare. Rather,
the practice of Buddhism strives to address each aspect of the process in a
holistic way. This requires not just a counter-psychology, but also a
counter-culture, a counter-economy, and counter-policies.

Buddhist Conceptions of a Desirable Society

In Buddhism, the prototype of this counter-civilization is known as the
Sangha—originally the monastic order, more broadly the community of
Buddhist believers. The early Sangha represented an attempt to replace
family and home by a brotherhood of wanderers; moreover, private prop-

127

erty was replaced by minimal possessions, hierarchy by equality, and coercion by cooperation. According to the disciplinary code of the monastic Sangha, any conflicts among the monks and nuns were to be resolved peacefully and democratically. In order to spread stability to society as a whole, the Sangha sought also to establish moral hegemony over the state and to teach nonviolence as an exemplary foundation of ethics.

In situations where these Buddhist ideals have been most nearly approximated, there has been an intimate triangular relationship between the Sangha, a king, and the people. The Sangha advises the ruler, guides him in the Dharma, and supports him in his administration of the state. In return, the king provides protection for the Sangha, ensuring optimum conditions for the pursuit of the Buddhist way. At its best, a Buddhist temple or monastery supports constant cultivation of mindfulness and also remains easily accessible to the people. Social contact enables the ethical and spiritual values of Buddhism to be transmitted to the culture at large. These early conceptions of the Sangha suggest that even a radically contemplative religion is not inherently insular, individualistic, or socially ineffective.

However, since the death of the Buddha some 2,500 years ago, the historical Sangha has been split vertically and horizontally by cultural, economic, and political conditions. In many countries, segments of the Sangha became dependent on state patronage for their preservation and expansion. The growth of monastic wealth and landholding was accompanied by the integration of the Sangha into society; often the priestly class became another sector of the elite, with its own social power, cultural influence, and selfish interests. The institutionalization of the Sangha was typically linked to state control, so that instead of holding the state to the ethics of nonviolence, the Sangha was increasingly called upon to rationalize violence and injustice.

These developments demonstrate that one of the largest obstacles to the implementation of religious principles is the mixing of religion and culture. Religion's impact on culture is not the issue that concerns us here; the problems arise when culture influences religion or is equated with religion. Among the distortions that result from cultural influences are religious sectarianism, literalism, and idolatry. How many times have such tendencies led to violence and killing in the name of religion? To take a recent example: in Sri Lanka, which claims to be a Buddhist state, there has been a massive outbreak of ethnic violence. Why has the Buddhist teaching of compassion and nonviolence apparently failed there? The Sinhalese Buddhists seem to have adopted a nationalist ideology based on racial concepts (despite the Buddha's explicit rejection of division by race). Because traditional Buddhist terms and categories of thought have not been translated into modern language and ways of thinking, the clergy and the laity in Sri Lanka have been unable to grasp the social implications of their own Buddhist teachings.

Early Buddhist political thought envisioned an ideal ruler, a world-conquering monarch, who subdued the earth through righteousness rather than war. A commitment to peace was one of the ten duties of such a king. Other qualities demanded of him were self-sacrifice for the people, honesty, gentleness, austerity, tolerance, generosity, freedom from enmity, and receptivity to the people's will. A direct link was made between a ruler's ethical standards and peace in the world. Not only did the ideal king prevent poverty and injustice domestically; his reign was also the model of a just and nonviolent transnational order. The power which allowed such a monarch to gain hegemony over all the kings of the four quarters stemmed from the establishment of righteousness in his own kingdom. Once the needs of all the people had been satisfied, a Wheel of Righteousness would begin to roll over the earth, peacefully eliciting the homage of lesser kings. Rather than interfering in the affairs of these other leaders, the world-conqueror would demand only that they uphold the cardinal Buddhist precepts in governing themselves and their countries.

Global Implications of the Buddhist Precepts

Many elements of the Buddhist tradition, however ancient they may be, are as germane today as they were in the era of Shakyamuni Buddha. For example, the basic ethical precepts in Buddhism are the vows to avoid killing, stealing, sexual misconduct, lying, and intoxication. In light of contemporary conditions, we find that the individual and social dimensions of these guidelines are inextricably linked.

The first precept, not to kill, naturally calls for the settling of internal and external conflict through nonviolent means. By extension, it would also entail a renunciation of the production and use of weapons, especially weapons that threaten all life on earth. Even if we succeed in avoiding a nuclear holocaust, the 1991 Gulf War showed that high-tech "conventional" weapons can kill more people more quickly than ever before. Our world is seriously deformed by the enormous resources being expended for the sake of annihilation. How we think, speak, and act in the ensuing decades will determine whether or not we can reassert control over the destructive forces we have unleashed.

For Buddhists, the first precept does not only mean to stop killing with weapons. It also means not to live luxuriously or consume wastefully while others are dying of starvation. Buddhists have traditionally expressed their respect for sentient life by opposing the slaughter of animals. Today, when the world faces recurring food crises, measures in meat-eating countries to discourage the breeding of animals for consumption would be doubly compassionate, not only toward the animals but also toward the humans who need the grains set aside for livestock.

At the same time, we must see how hunger is caused by the unequal economic and power structures that do not allow food to go where it is needed, even when the needy are the producers themselves. One key component of these inequitable systems is the economic burden of the arms race that preoccupies many industrialized nations. In 1980 the Brandt Commission reported:

> There is a moral link between the vast spending on arms and the disgracefully low spending on measures to remove hunger and ill-health in the Third World. The program of the World Health Organization to abolish malaria is short of funds; it is estimated that it will eventually cost about US$450 million—which represents only one-thousandth of the world's annual military spending.[1]

A decade later, this terrible discrepancy remains. The statistics on global starvation and malnutrition are so awful to contemplate that we push them out of our minds. About a fifth of the world's population suffers from malnourishment. Thirty-five thousand to forty thousand people die of hunger *every day*, most of them children. In two years, hunger kills more people than the total number of casualties in World War I and World War II.

Building a peaceful world and establishing a just international economic order are interdependent. Most forms of violence—imperialist, civil, and interpersonal—stem from collective drives for economic resources and political power. An episode in the Buddhist scriptures illustrates this connection in terms of Indian society at the time. About five years after the Buddha gained enlightenment, he went back to his hometown and found his mother's tribe, the Koliyans, and his father's tribe, the Shakyans, on the verge of war. The dispute had been triggered when Shakyan and Koliyan farmers could not decide who should be first to divert the Rohini River into their fields. Both sides insisted that their crops would ripen with a single watering, and then the other side would be welcome to divert the river. The farmers began to insult one another, and tensions escalated. Just as the tribes' warriors rushed out to avenge the insults, the Buddha stepped in. The warriors dropped their weapons in embarrassment as their enlightened kinsman questioned them about the cause of the quarrel. When he discovered that the dispute was about water, he asked both sides whether water was worth as much as the lives of the fathers and sons who served as warriors. They answered that warriors were beyond price, and he said, "Then it is not fitting that because of a little water you should destroy warriors who are beyond price."[2]

While contemporary controversies may be more complex, the inter-weaving of greed and aggression persists in the military-industrial complexes of many nations, large and small. Countless politicians, media figures, generals, intellectuals, managers, technicians, stockholders, and others are dependent on the existence or even the threat of conflict. As President Eisenhower warned, the ideological and cultural power of the military-industrial complex slowly poisons American life. The merchants of death who advertise paranoia and hate will reap their profits at an incalculable social cost.

Economic justice—the broad social application of not stealing—is bound up with what Buddhists call "right livelihood," a job that does not cause harm to others. Obviously, the manufacture or trading of weapons is not right livelihood. A peaceful society may need certain weapons to defend itself or channel its internal conflicts, but society's parasitic dependence on the war process is clearly wrong. Economic peace conversion (turning tank factories into tractor factories, or Star Wars projects into space colonization projects) should be a common aspiration of citizens everywhere. Not taking responsibility for the exploitation and violence involved in one's economic system is nearly as serious as being a thief or a murderer oneself. So what can we do? The answers will differ according to one's circumstances. To live a life of voluntary simplicity, out of compassion for all beings, is a meaningful way to set oneself against the unethical tendencies built into the status quo. A life guided by *ahiṃsā* may require the renunciation of fame, profit, and power as worthwhile goals. But even those forms of abstention may not be enough, unless one is also working to overturn the structures that compel others to live in poverty involuntarily.

The third precept repudiates improper sexuality. In contemporary terms, Buddhist sexual ethics must address the global structures that facilitate male domination and the exploitation of women. Cycles of patriarchal greed and ignorance have been with us a long time, and they generate violence in many different ways. For instance, the anthropologist Marvin Harris has studied tribal cultures that practice female infanticide, and he discovered that one of the functions of war for those tribes is to kill off the resulting surplus of males. In a vicious cycle, that warfare in turn promotes the valuation of male strength and prowess, attitudes that lead back to the starvation of baby girls and the favoring of boys.[3] Like its tribal antecedents, modern militarism is still associated with patriarchy, and militaristic political forces oppose women's liberation.

In most societies, violence against women is related to their economic position; when economically inferior women are also members of oppressed classes or races, the persecution is exacerbated. Rape, pornography, and prostitution are the inevitable outcome of systems that objectify women's bodies, which are reduced to commodities on the market. Sex tourism is a common phenomenon in my country, Thailand, where there may now be more prostitutes than monks. Increasingly, Thai and Filipino prostitution is also being exported to Japan, Hong Kong, and Western Europe. Such developments bring suffering to all those involved—the collective karma of male dominance limits men's abilities to achieve spiritual liberation as much as it stifles the potential of women. In contrast, Buddhist practice seeks to develop full human beings, free from socially learned "masculine" and "feminine" patterns of thought, speech, and behavior.

The fourth precept, to speak the truth, has obvious relevance for everyone working toward peace and justice. Some Americans in the antiwar movement have characterized their role as "speaking truth to power." For the exiled Tibetans described in Robert Thurman's essay, "words of truth" are believed to be mightier than any army. Buddhism teaches that ultimate truth may be unknowable and inexpressible; those who humbly accept this mysterious tenet can use it to undercut their own dogmatism, racism, and nationalism.

The forces of violence and domination perpetuate ideologies, values, and patterns of information that condition our understanding of the world, often unconsciously. For example, news coverage of an ongoing war almost always validates the viewpoint of the military. When mass media use falsehoods and distortions to capture people's minds, they also create many desires that cannot easily be fulfilled. In underdeveloped nations, advertising often rejects indigenous culture in the name of progress and modernization. In Thailand, for instance, the marketing of Coca Cola and Pepsi Cola has made villagers ashamed to offer a visitor the traditional drink of rainwater—they now feel they must offer something in a bottle, even though each bottle costs them one day of their earnings. Consumer culture works hand-in-glove with greed and lust, arising out of delusion and ignorance. The way to perceive and break free of the systematic duplicity that surrounds us it to practice truth-speaking in our public and private lives, and to do it collectively whenever possible.

The spiritual path enables one to acknowledge truthfully the presence of one's own violent and greedy tendencies, and to recognize the emptiness of the stereotyped enemy. Though men have repeatedly rationalized their aggressions with the fiction that their enemies were not even human, today we can no longer afford to fall prey to the mass projections of militaristic propaganda. For a Buddhist, being in touch with the truth is being grounded in a deep, critical doubt about beliefs and prejudices, including one's own. The practice of meditation illuminates the arising of illusion; a person who has seen this process has no choice but to hold his or her opinions more loosely. According to the *Vimalakīrti Sūtra*, it is the duty of bodhisattvas to devote themselves "to all the strange sects of the world," so that "those who have attached themselves to dogmatic views" can be converted to ecumenical tolerance.[4]

The fifth precept's vow to "abstain from intoxicants that cloud the mind" and to encourage others similarly to abstain has become a complex proposition in today's world. When we attempt to overturn the forces which foster alcoholism and drug addiction, we find that they too are linked to questions of international justice and peace. In many cases, Third World farmers grow heroin, coca, coffee, or tobacco because the economic system makes it impossible for them to grow rice or vegetables profitably. Those who act as their middlemen, whether state officials in Latin America or guerrilla leaders on the Burmese border, are frequently pseudopolitical bandits of some sort. Full-scale wars have been fought by governments in order to maintain the drug trade (England's Opium War against China is but one example). When peasants are forced to plant export crops of coffee or tea for Northerners' legal consumption, or when American-made cigarettes are intensively marketed to Third World consumers, that too is economic violence involving intoxicants.

Drug abuse and drug-related crime arise most often in the crippled cultures or subcultures spawned by unemployment, unequal distribution of wealth, and alienation from work. The use of American armed forces to fight the drug trade is just as misguided as the Russian campaign against worker alcoholism—both address symptoms instead of causes. If government leaders do not recognize their own addictive behavior involving alcohol or prescription drugs, if they do not work to alleviate the despair that makes drugs attractive, and if they continue to support regimes that profit from large-scale drug traffic, how can they expect symbolic measures such as a "war on drugs" to succeed?

Buddhism in the Modern World

Whatever belief-system or faith we favor, we need to study other ideologies and religions in order to appreciate their strengths. What we can accept from other systems of thought and belief, we should accept. What we cannot accept, we need not blame or attack. The same goes for modern knowledge: we should know how to master it without being mastered by it.

Science and technology, so dominant in contemporary Western culture, are not necessarily detrimental to religion, but religion must prove itself able to influence them. Because science and technology are concerned with material matters, they have built-in limitations. Buddhism teaches that there are two kinds of truth: relative and higher. The first applies to the material realm, the truth of things that can be observed. Western science has progressed enormously in understanding this material world, but its contribution does not extend much beyond that. Even scientists have come to see that on the level of materiality there is no permanence, no absolute existence. For the science of higher truth, one must turn to religion.

The Buddha never suggested that people ought to reject material things. What must be renounced is the desire to own or hold onto things, not the things themselves. Inanimate objects, fortunately, will not form attachments to human beings! A number of people harbor the misconception that Buddhism advocates poverty; they miss the deeper message about contentment, few wants, or nonindulgence. But poverty per se is not extolled in Buddhist teaching; on the contrary, possession of wealth by a king or an average householder can be praiseworthy. What is considered important in Buddhism is how the wealth is gained and how it is used. A good Buddhist layman, who has become prosperous in an honest and lawful way, devotes much or most of his wealth to support the Sangha and to alleviate the suffering of others. Not being attached to wealth or infatuated with it, he enjoys spiritual freedom.

Capitalism exploits religion one way, communism another. Though both ideologies claim to organize societies to benefit mankind, their overemphasis of materialism and secular development betrays a superficial understanding of humanity. When priests or religious leaders assume the role of capitalists (for example, by promoting their churches or dealing with large amounts of money), they often become attached to their own wealth and fame. Before long, they are sacrificing their ideals in order to support the power structure and preserve the status quo. As for communism, the effects of its hostility to religion are well-known. China has not only crushed Tibetan Buddhism, it has also produced a new generation of Chinese who are entirely ignorant of their country's great Buddhist heritage.

World suffering is too immense for any one country, religion, or group to solve. And yet, paradoxical as it may seem, the way out of our predicament is for all of us recognize that the problems on earth are our own personal problems and our own personal responsibility. For those in the northern hemisphere, this responsibility is immediate. Unless the citizens of the richest nations seriously change their lifestyles, and do it soon, there is little hope. A mother in Minnesota must come to see a famine in Calcutta as her own agony; a shopkeeper in Germany must experience the suppression of freedom in Burma as his own imprisonment.

The defense of human rights takes ethical precedence over national sovereignty. Most people are able to accept this tenet when addressing an obvious abuse such as apartheid. In that case, the claim by the minority whites that the world should not interfere in South Africa's internal affairs is not seen as a legitimate application of national sovereignty. By the same token, other regimes that deny their citizens full, free, and equal participation in the decision-making that affects their lives should thereby lose international recognition of their legitimacy. Even minorities in democratic societies can suffer injustices that may call for external sanctions. Will the world be more just and peaceful if we accept an "outlaw" nation's sovereignty or if we violate it in the interests of compassion? The ethical judgments are often as complex as the political ones. Actually, global interdependence means that we are no longer faced with the question "Shall we intervene in that nation's affairs?" Especially for citizens of the North, a better question is: "How shall we change our present political, economic, and cultural involvement in that country?" As always, we must exhaust all possible nonviolent responses.

In Buddhism, one's individual karmic burden is considered a precious gift, for only by working with that karma is there an opportunity for liberation. The same principle applies on a larger scale. However intractable our national and international problems may appear, they contain the seeds of their resolution. Unless our work for peace and justice is connected to the social reality of collective karma, it will simply be utopian idealism.

Contemporary Buddhist internationalism envisions institutions that are configured to represent the interests of human beings rather than nation-states. Consider the United Nations, for example. The peripheral status of the U.N. could first be addressed by strengthening the authority of its representatives (while lowering their hunger for privilege). By moving toward a true world parliament elected directly by a world citizenry, the organization would be more likely to make decisions that best reflect the common interests of humanity. The current body might be maintained as an upper house, and then a new 500-member lower house could be established, representing electorates of ten million people each.

If the deliberations of the U.N. achieved greater legitimacy, its international conflict-resolution mechanisms could be expanded. Its resolutions might then have real impact, and the secretary-general might have genuine influence as a peacemaker. There will eventually have to be some kind of global disarmament administration, probably connected with an international satellite system to monitor weapons stockpiles. Some means of dealing with violations will be necessary; a precedent exists in the U.S.-Soviet Joint Consultative Commission created in the SALT negotiations. The U.N. or its successor could also administer a strengthened international judiciary system and a permanent peacekeeping force recruited independently of existing armies. In the realm of economics, similar cooperative responses must be developed to deal with the transnationalization of capital. Leaders of transnational corporations (TNCs) make decisions that shape the lives of millions of people, yet those who are affected have little or no voice in corporate policy. International labor organizations have made some attempt to address the impact of TNCs, but governments must also join together to tax, regulate, and sanction these giant companies.

We already have eloquent documents that express our common yearnings for international cooperation. Consider the preamble of UNESCO's constitution, which declares:

> That since wars begin in the minds of men, it is in the minds of men that the defences of peace must be constructed. . . .
> That a peace based exclusively upon the political and economic arrangements of governments would not be a peace which could secure the unanimous, lasting, and sincere support of the peoples of the world, and that the peace must therefore be founded, if it is not to fail, upon the intellectual and moral solidarity of mankind.[5]

If the economic interdependence of nations provides the carrot for world federalism, the threat of mutual destruction surely provides the stick.

Peace and freedom are so interdependent that the causal relation works in either direction: without freedom, there can be no real peace; without peace, there can be no true freedom. It may be helpful in this regard to clarify the various types of "freedom." The first is freedom from the fundamental insecurities and dangers that threaten existence—poverty, disease, drought, famine, and so on. At the second level is social freedom, made possible by communities that promote tolerance and benevolence while rejecting oppression and exploitation. The third and last is the freedom of one's inner life—freedom from mental suffering, greed, hatred, and delusion. Without freedom from want and oppression, people cannot be expected to appreciate more sublime forms of personal liberation. At the same time, those who have tasted psychological/spiritual emancipation can work most effectively to alleviate the deprivation and exploitation that others experience.

Buddhist teachings are not concerned with the private destiny of the individual, but with something much wider: the whole realm of sentient existence, the totality of consciousness. Accordingly, social and political matters receive considerable attention in the Pali canon of early Buddhism. Unless Western Buddhists appreciate the broader dimensions of the tradition, their involvement with Buddhism will not enable them to cure the disease of extreme individualism. Religion itself has no permanence of form—the basic principles may be unchanging, but practice continuously evolves. Representatives of Asian Buddhism who are teaching in the West must be ever mindful of the positive and negative aspects of their own cultures; they cannot expect students newly attracted to Buddhism to adopt its cultural accretions as well. Once Buddhism establishes deeper roots in the West, European and American Buddhists will undoubtedly transcend the present horizon of understanding. Those who are able to synthesize insight and action will have a real opportunity to contribute to the world.

Many of the aims and proposals offered here may seem difficult or unattainable, but they are not beyond our human ability. Even in the past few years, we have witnessed several important developments around the world that never seemed possible until they happened. To oppose those who kill and oppress, one must not only have a mind free of hostility; one must also be skilled in dealing with the complexities of the social system. Twenty-five centuries ago the Buddha taught people to face and surmount the reality of human existence—the essential problems of pain, loss, suffering, sickness, and death. Isn't that still our task today? By building up communities of people with inner spiritual strength, moral courage, and concerned awareness of the world, Buddhists and non-Buddhists have already begun to restructure consciousness and reconstitute society for the future benefit of humanity.

Notes

I am grateful to James Hughes for his contributions to an earlier draft of this essay.

1. Willy Brandt, ed., *North-South, A Programme for Survival: Report of the Independent Commission on International Development Issues* (Cambridge: MIT Press, 1980), 117–18.
2. John A. McConnell, "The Rohini Conflict and the Buddha's Intervention," in *Radical Conservatism: Buddhism in the Contemporary World* (Bangkok: Thai Inter-Religious Commission for Development, 1990), 200–208.
3. Marvin Harris, *Death, Sex, and Fertility* (New York: Columbia University Press, 1987), 55–62.
4. Robert A. F. Thurman, trans., *The Holy Teaching of Vimalakīrti* (University Park: Pennsylvania State University Press, 1976), 69.
5. Walter H. C. Leaves, *UNESCO: Purpose, Progress, Prospects* (Bloomington: Indiana University Press, 1957), 415.

Contributors

CHRISTOPHER CHAPPLE (Ph.D., Fordham University) is Associate Professor of Theology at Loyola Marymount University. He is the author of *Karma and Creativity* and the cotranslator of *Yoga Sūtras of Patañjali*.

CYNTHIA ELLER (Ph.D., University of Southern California) is an adjunct member of the Philosophy Department at Fairleigh Dickinson University. She is completing a book on American conscientious objectors in World War II.

LUIS O. GÓMEZ (Ph.D., Yale University) is Professor of Asian Languages and Cultures at the University of Michigan. He is the coeditor of several books, including *Barabudur: History and Significance of a Religious Monument* and *Prajñāpāramitā and Related Systems*.

KENNETH KRAFT (Ph.D., Princeton University) is Associate Professor of Religion Studies at Lehigh University. He is the author of *Eloquent Zen: Daitō and Early Japanese Zen* and the editor of *Zen: Tradition and Transition*.

GENE SHARP (D. Phil., Oxford University) is Senior Scholar-in-Residence at the Albert Einstein Institution. He has written *The Politics of Nonviolent Action*, *Gandhi as a Political Strategist*, *Making Europe Unconquerable*, and *Civilian-Based Defense: A Post-Military Weapons System*.

SULAK SIVARAKSA is Director of the Santi Pracha Dhamma Institute and President of the Thai Inter-Religious Commission for Development. He has been a visiting professor at Cornell and other American universities. His books include *Religion and Development, Seeds of Peace: A Buddhist Vision for Renewing Society,* and *Siamese Resurgence*.

DONALD SWEARER (Ph.D., Princeton University) is Professor of Religion at Swarthmore College. Among the books he has authored or edited, the most recent are *For the Sake of the World: Christian and Buddhist Monasticism* and *Me and Mine: Selected Essays of Bhikkhu Buddhadasa.*

ROBERT A. F. THURMAN (Ph.D., Harvard University) is Professor of Religion at Columbia University. His translations include *The Holy Teaching of Vimalakīrti* and *The Central Philosophy of Tibet: A Study and Translation of Jey Tsong Khapa's Essence of True Eloquence.*

Index

Abe, Masao, 103
abstention, and nonviolence, 2–3, 33, 35, 37, 42, 45, 46, 131
Ācārāṅga Sūtra, 51
accommodation, by opposition, 122
action meditation model of nonviolence, 104
actions, 95; effects of, 13, 38, 87, 93, 96. *See also* interdependence; karma
activism, 5, 104; and self-cultivation, 105
African National Congress, 118
aggression, 112, 113–115, 120–121; greed and, 78, 131. *See also* war
ahiṃsā (nonviolence), 31–46, 92, 112, 121, 131; etymology of word, 50–51; Jain vows of, 50–51. *See also* nonviolence
AIDS patients, hospice for, 15, 16
Aitken, Robert, 15, 23, 93, 95, 106; *The Mind of Clover*, 94
Ajatasattu, 67–68
ajīva (nonliving forms), 50
Akbar, Emperor, 52
alcohol, 51
alcoholism, 133
Amitābha Buddha, 77–78
anattā (nonself), 64, 94
anger, 12, 35, 78, 93, 103, 121. *See also* hatred
animal nature, of humans, 115
animals, 6, 115; birth as, 52–53; human sacrifice for, 53; nonviolence to, 49–60; protection of, 55–57; in

scientific research, 6, 57–60; slaughter of, 6, 129; stories about, 40, 52, 53; treatment in Buddhism, 52–54
animal sacrifice, 34; Jains' protest against, 51–52
Aniruddha, 66
apparent reality, 81, 133
Arab oil embargo, 117
arahant (worthy one), 68
Ariyaratne, A.T., 69
arms race, 14, 129, 130; opposition to, 12
Asaṅga, 6, 78
Asian Cultural Forum on Development, 69
Aśoka, King, 4, 32, 33–35, 55, 64–66, 75, 85
attention, continuous full (*sampajañña*), 70
Aung San Suu Kyi, 25
Avadāna-kalpalatā, 53
Avadāna Śataka, 53
Avalokiteśvara, 77, 81–82, 86, 88, 89
Avataṃsaka Sūtra, 46
awareness, 7, 19, 70, 95, 127; of breath, 19–20

balanced state of nature, 70
Bangladesh, 25
Beijing, massacre in (1989), 7, 122
being peace, 4, 19
bhikkhu (monk), 54. *See also* monk(s)
Bimbisara, 67

141

universal harmony, 31, 82
universal monarch (*cakkavatti*), 66, 129
upekkhā (equanimity), 64
uposatha (recitation of moral code), 36, 37, 39, 67–68
U.S.-Soviet Joint Consultative Commission, 135

Vajrayana Buddhism, 12, 81, 87
Van Hanh Buddhist University (Saigon), 18
vegetarianism, 6, 34, 36, 51, 52, 57
Vessantara, Prince, 66–67, 75
victory, 99, 122; of God, 99
Vietnam, 22, 25–26, 99, 112; Buddhist monks in, 26
Vietnam War, 4, 14, 18, 98; Thich Nhat Hanh and, 11, 22
Vimalakīrti Sūtra, 82, 132–133
Vinaya (monastic code), 3, 5, 36, 46, 64, 128. *See also* precepts
violence, 7, 22, 38, 58, 78, 89, 99–100, 114; alternatives to, 114–123; defining, 78; political, Buddhists and, 111–114; resorting to, 5; types of, 51, 78, 130; against women, 131–132. *See also* nonviolence

vipassanā (insight) meditation, 15
Viviano, Benedict, 96
vow(s): of Avalokiteśvara, 77, 78, 88–89; of Jainism, 50–51

Walesa, Lech, 120
walking meditation, 20
Wang Yang-ming, 3
war, 8, 64, 130, 131, 136; justified, 113
wealth, 134
weapons, 85, 129. *See also* arms race; nuclear weapons
Weber, Max, 3
Weimer Republic, 117
Wheel of Righteousness, 129
women, exploitation of, 131–132
world: creation of, 83; and self, 44, 91–92
World Health Organization, 130
world peace, 2, 14, 18, 20, 105, 127

Yoder, John Howard, 97, 99

zazen (Zen meditation), 103. *See also* meditation
Zen Community of New York, 16